ENNIS AND NANCY HAM LIBRARY
ROCHESTER COLLEGE
800 WEST AVON ROAD
ROCHESTER HILLS, MI 48307

ROCHESTER COLLEGE
MUIRHEAD LIBRARY
800 WEST AVON ROAD
ROCHESTER HILLS MI 48307

PN
4888
.O25
Y68
2001

MEDIA BIAS:
How Political Prejudice Distorts The News

Frank M. Young

Information Products
Lompoc, California

February 15, 2001

Copyright © 2000 by Frank M. Young

All rights reserved

No part of this book may be reproduced in any form without permission in writing from the publisher.

Published by Information Products
PO Box 2260, Lompoc, California 93438
Manufactured in the United States of America

First Edition
Second Printing

ISBN 0-9674277-0-3

ACKNOWLEDGMENTS

Now I understand why authors dedicate books to their significant others. That's because they are subjected to all the preliminary versions of the manuscript. Even though they have heard an idea a hundred times, they listen to the latest nuance as if it were bold new inspiration. My wife Anita Friedman did more than that. Her knowledge of psychology proved invaluable to my investigation of the social psychology of prejudice. There are others who deserve recognition.

For years, I would say, "I'll get my book into print this year." A cadre of unbelievers grew among my friends and acquaintances. However, there was a small band of faithful who always know that I would finish and publish this book. My friends Herbert and Sally Jennings never doubted that they would live to see a copy of my book. Among the believers, I give special thanks to Dr. Larry Riemer who was my ghost editor. His encouragement and excellent suggestions helped to shape the book. The detailed review of my manuscript by Ms Helen Thomas morphed it into the first smooth draft.

Finally, I wish to acknowledge the election of William Jefferson Clinton to the presidency. The first draft of the book was written when George Bush was president. The national media at that time was in full opposition mode. Press coverage of Bush oozed with partisan contempt and the manuscript reflected only the opposition dimension of political reporting. With the election of a Democrat, I had the opportunity to observe the press in its supportive mode. When Clinton perpetrated scandals (real and imagined), the elite press worked mightily to control the shape and flow of the news in a brazen effort to limit the public relations damage to their man in the White House.

TABLE OF CONTENTS

INTRODUCTION .... -i-

POLITICAL PREJUDICE 1
    MORAL SUPERIORITY 3
    POLITICAL STEREOTYPING 6
    POLITICAL INTOLERANCE 8
    KEY CONCEPT 14
    DISCUSSION 15
    END NOTES 16

PERCEPTION BIAS 20
    LOADED LABELS 24
    CONNECTING THE DOTS 27
    HANDLING RAW NEWS INFORMATION 33
    A FUNDAMENTAL PERCEPTION ERROR 41
    SUMMARY 42
    DISCUSSION 43
    END NOTES 45

PARTISAN BIAS 48
    REPUBLICANS DON'T ACCOMPLISH MUCH 52
    DEMOCRATS HAVE ALTRUISTIC MOTIVES 53
    DEMOCRATS USUALLY TELL THE TRUTH 54
    REPUBLICANS PLAY DIRTY 57
    REPUBLICANS RARELY DESERVE ANY RESPECT 60
    SUMMARY 61
    DISCUSSION 62
    END NOTES 63

IDEOLOGICAL BIAS 65
    THE WELFARE STATE IS GOOD 67
    THE COLD WAR WAS NOT WORTH FIGHTING 71
    JEWS OCCUPY ISRAEL AND OPPRESS ARABS 73
    THERE IS NO RIGHT TO OWN A FIREARM 74
    HOWEVER, WOMEN HAVE A RIGHT TO ABORTION .. 75
    THE ENVIRONMENTALISTS ARE RIGHT 75
    CONSERVATIVE VOICE 76
    SUMMARY 77

| DISCUSSION 78
| END NOTES 80

POLITICAL FAVORITISM 83
| A PARTISAN DOUBLE STANDARD 84
| ATTACK JOURNALISM 86
| FLACK JOURNALISM 88
| DISCUSSION 92
| END NOTES 93

THE BATTLE FOR PUBLIC OPINION 95
| THE ELITE PRESS as POLITICAL INTEREST GROUP ... 97
| POLITICAL ADVERTISING 98
| THE POWER OF THE PRESS 100
| THE WINNING IMPRESSION 101
| KEY IDEA 106
| SUMMARY 106
| DISCUSSION 107
| END NOTES 108

PARTISAN SPIN 111
| EXAMPLE: A Fictional Air Fare 113
| EXAMPLE: Medicare "Cuts" versus "Savings" 115
| AGENDA SETTING 117
| EXAMPLE: The 1984 Presidential Campaign 119
| PRIMING PUBLIC OPINION 120
| THE BLAME GAME 122
| APPROVAL AND DISAPPROVAL 124
| VERBAL SPIN 126
| Loaded Words 127
| Twisted Words 128
| EXAMPLE: Twisting Speaker Gingrich 129
| Abusive Use of Vague Sources 131
| Ringer Sources 132
| SUMMARY 133
| DISCUSSION 134
| END NOTES 135

SCANDALMONGERING 138
| THE TYPICAL SUCCESSFUL SCANDAL 141

SCANDAL PERSPECTIVES 143
PRESS COVERAGE OF SCANDALS 145
    Covering Democratic Targets 150
PROFESSOR ANITA HILL VERSUS MS. PAULA JONES
.... 155
SUMMARY 158
DISCUSSION 160
END NOTES 161

REINVENTING JOURNALISM 162
    AUTHORITARIAN TRUTH 162
    THE REAL TRUTH 164
    DEMOCRATIC TRUTH 166
    JOURNALISTIC TRUTH 167
    NEWS AS A QUALITY PROCESS 168
        Pluralistic 169
        Timely 169
        Reliable 170
        Representative 171
        Constantly Correct The Record 172
    SELF-POLICING 173
    CITIZEN JOURNALISM 175
    POSTSCRIPT 176
    END NOTES 177

GLOSSARY 178

IDEOLOGY 185

ANNOTATED BIBLIOGRAPHY 189

INDEX 193

INTRODUCTION

Journalists claim that their political opinions do not influence the way they gather and produce the news. They claim they have the ability to set their opinions aside when they come to work. Accusations of bias are glibly blown off. The words of Mr. Tom Brokaw, anchor for the *NBC Nightly News*, typify the attitude.

At a 1996 National Press Club luncheon, Brokaw was asked, "A recent poll said that more than 89 percent of journalists voted for Clinton in 1992, 7 percent for Bush. Can you respond to complaints from many Republicans, including Senator Robert Dole, that the press does not lean our way. If they are right what should the press do about it?" Brokaw responded,

> "I think you would have a hard time finding anybody in the Clinton White House, right now, who believes that the press is leaning in the way of this president. I mean it's a common complaint among those people who are in the public arena. We wouldn't have it any other way. We don't intend to lean one way or the other. We hope to lean toward, as much as we can, finding the facts about what's going on, on any given day, and over a course of time.
>
> I do think as well, in the case of Bob Dole, when you are behind, and you are trying to get something going, it's one of the ways you can mobilize your troops. Someone said to me on the way in here today, in fact a couple of people have, that there's not enough outrage out there about the FBI files, for example, that have ended up in the Clinton administration, in the Clinton White House, at the moment. It's not because the press hasn't publicized this. It was a major point of discussion on Tim Russert's "Meet The Press" on Sunday. The other Sunday talk shows, it was a major piece last night by Bryan Williams. It was covered on NBC on Friday night, when we first heard about this.

So there's been an extraordinary amount of exposure of the fact that these FBI files, in fact, were taken from the FBI and left in the White House by what they're calling a low-level Army functionary. Now, it's up to the political process to respond as it will.

And that's what our job has been in the past and that's what it will be in the future. I don't think that anyone who is in office or is seeking office in this country, would go to a microphone, privately or publicly, and say, "You know I don't have a lot else going for me, but the press is on my side."

He was then asked, "But are there any other reasons why the media is perceived as biased?" Brokaw sharpened his ridicule of the question.

"You know Jim [Lehrer of the Public Broadcasting Service (PBS)] and I agree on almost everything. We both married our trophy wives the first time around. We both have been the beneficiaries of having four extraordinary strong gifted women, who had no hesitation about putting us in our place, the moment we walked through the door. We could get a lot of attention under the bright lights and from all the attention in the places where we work, until we arrive home. And then there was a kind of leveling influence on the part of our families.

And I think it's fair to say, that given that common of experience, it's fair to say that we have a common attitude about this business of 'bias in the press.' The old cliche that we've all used over the years is that bias, like beauty, is 'in the eye of the beholder.' We're out there on the cutting edge of change, on a daily basis."

The claim that bias "like beauty" is in the eye of the beholder, is not supported by the evidence. Research in the field of psychology provides ample reason to believe that biases corrupt the perceptions and thinking of all people, including journalists. So, in the following pages I will show how the Liberal biases of leading journalists distort the news.

Chapter 1

POLITICAL PREJUDICE

Political prejudice is perhaps the last form of socially acceptable bigotry. Partisans routinely glamorize themselves as the true servants of "the people" while denigrating their opposition as enemies of society. This pernicious prejudice characterizes political speech everywhere, from the political campaign trail to the evening news that covers it. Liberal journalists who would never dream of using a racial or gender stereotype have no such reluctance when it comes to political stereotypes.

The national press often tags political Conservatives as "insensitive," "mean" and "selfish."[1] If something bad happens, journalists lead news consumers to believe that Conservatives are to blame. If religious Conservatives try to enter politics, journalists suggest that it is wrong for them to do so. However, when religious Liberals try to enter politics they are praised for responding a high calling. This intolerance of Conservatives not only dominates the editorial pages of leading newspapers, it materializes on the evening news as proven fact.[2]

The dictionary suggests that a *fact* is a piece of information which represents objective reality. That is, a fact is real. A fact has actual existence. Okay. But, how do you know that a body of information, like a news story, is factual? That's the problem. Unless God personally tells you that something is true, you have to rely on your own observation or the word of someone you trust. With that in mind, let me define a fact as *information which has been verified as true by a reliable observer in accordance with an acceptable standard*. If it passes that test, information consumers assume that the "facts" accurately represent reality.

However, people have a tendency to skip the verification process and leap to conclusions. People tend to prejudge information. Such prejudgment is, by definition, *prejudice*. Racial prejudice is a prejudgment of a person based solely on race. A sexist judgement is one made solely on gender. That is, the racial or sexist bigot attributes traits and abilities to a whole group of people based solely on their race or sex. The word "prejudice" usually connotes an unjustified opinion about a person based on race, religion, national origin, sex or physical handicap.

Note that a person can prejudge anything - another person, an idea, an issue, a country, a philosophy - thus suggesting a general definition of the word. *A prejudice is an opinion, not easily deduced from information in the public domain, yet asserted as if it were proven fact.* Put another way, a prejudice is a fiction which is treated as fact. Note that unproven opinions, unsubstantiated beliefs and convenient fictions are all forms of prejudice.

We often use fictions in a benign fashion. They help us to understand the world. It is just not possible to know, with certainty, everything we need to know in order to make life's decisions. So, we make it up. We have no choice. We have to fill the information gaps with our unproven opinions and useful fictions. Thus, prejudice is a necessary characteristic of the thought process.

However, most prejudices are not offensive. For instance, I have always been prejudiced in favor of female brunettes. I attribute all manner of unproven wonderful qualities to them. This notion is not easily deduced from information in the public domain. I have even acted on that belief. The consequences of such prejudices are usually benign. Most people can live with them.

We usually call these benign prejudices, preferences. What we normally call prejudices are actually *offensive prejudices.* Prejudices based on traits like race, gender, physical capability or national origin are offensive. The essence of offensive prejudice is the prejudgment that "those people" are very likely inferior because of their membership in some out-group.

Many people hold their prejudices loosely and will at some point listen to logic and reason. However, others become unduly fond of their mental stopgap measures. Even when there is ample evidence that a prejudice has been proven wrong, bigots will tenaciously cling to it. A bigot does not simply hold a prejudice; a bigot is devoted to his prejudice. A bigot is loyal to the idea that his group is superior to other groups. A bigot insists on believing the best of his own in-group and the worst of those out-groups regardless of facts to the contrary.[3]

It should be noted that many bigots can appear quite reasonable. Bigots may be nice well-meaning people. Bigots may not use obviously prejudiced language. Bigots may even change their minds about some minor characteristic of an out-group. Bigots can also be aware of important exceptions to their rules of prejudice.

Racial bigotry has been well studied and most of us think we know it, when we see it. But what does the political version look like? To start with, political prejudice works just like any other kind. Instead of thinking they are better than someone of another race, religion or nationality, political bigots think they are better than other political groups. Most politicians and activists are part of some political in-group such as Liberal Democrats, Conservative Republicans, the National Organization for Women or the National Rifle Association. Political groups perceive themselves as good people trying to make the world a better place, while viewing their partisan opponents as foreign, strange and inferior Republicans think they are superior to Democrats and vice versa. Conservatives think they are better than Liberals.

Partisans often exhibit an attitude of native superiority. Each partisan camp sees itself as the only one competent to lead the country. Political opponents are perceived as out of touch with reality and therefore unfit to govern. Partisans think they have a superior understanding of government, the people, foreign affairs, civil unrest, war, peace, poverty and economics. But most importantly, partisans see themselves as morally superior to enemy out-groups.

MORAL SUPERIORITY

People tend to think that the beliefs and tastes common to their own in-group are superior. Group norms are seen as the correct ones for themselves and good for people everywhere. This attitude is often accompanied by *a tendency to glorify the in-group while denigrating out-groups.*[4] There is a tendency to view the in-group as the center of the universe and to fear "outsiders." Sociologists usually refer to such attitudes as "ethnocentrism." Like their ethnocentric cousins, partisans see themselves as the center of the universe leading them to believe that they are morally superior to political out-groups.

Thus, members of political groupings like Democrats, Republicans, Liberals and Conservatives tend to perceive their vision of America as the only authentic one. Each group thinks that it speaks for "the people." All partisans think their perception of what is good is shared by all decent people everywhere.[5] Moral superiority is also a trait of the Liberal news.

Consider talk news programs where a journalist moderates a discussion with several panelists on current issues in the news. The moderator will typically introduce the token Conservative with a label like "Conservative activist," "Conservative Economist" or "Republican operative." However, the Liberal panelists will be introduced as an "economist," an "expert" or an "activist." By attaching the partisan label to the Conservative, the journalist is alerting news consumers to an outsider whose words are suspect. And, by omitting the partisan labels of the other panelists, the moderator is identifying them as good in-group people whose words can be taken at face value.

Moral superiority may surface in the way people talk. Journalists often talk as if all good people were just like them, Liberal Democrats. For instance, journalists talk about women as if all women were Liberal-minded feminists. News coverage of the United States Senate hearing to confirm Judge Clarence Thomas to the Supreme Court of the United States in 1991 provided a good example.

EXAMPLE: Reporting on "The Year of the Woman"

In the spring of 1991, Republican President George Bush nominated Judge Clarence Thomas to fill the Supreme Court vacancy left by retiring Justice Thurgood Marshall. Judge Thomas is African-American and a Conservative Republican. A high profile Conservative African-American is exactly what Liberals did not want. It would make it difficult to equate Conservatism with racism. The Liberal wing of the Democratic party declared war. Bitter partisan combat followed. As usual, the press sided with the Democrats and did its best to mobilize public opinion against the Republicans.

The first battle took place during the Senate hearing to confirm or deny the appointment of Judge Thomas to the Supreme Court. After the Senate hearing, it looked as if his confirmation as a Supreme Court justice was assured. At that point, Professor Anita Hill came forward and accused him of improper sexual conduct. In essence, she accused him of "talking dirty" to her. Her testimony before the Senate Judiciary Committee was a national event.

Republicans seeking to defend Thomas had tough questions for his accuser, Professor Hill. Democrats who wanted to sink his nomination were conveniently offended at these tough questions. Democrats apparently thought if they were offended, all decent people were offended. The reasoning goes as follows. All women must have been offended. Women were going to fight back against this outrage. A new wave of political activism was ignited. Women would run for public office in record numbers. Thus, the political fiction called "The Year of the Woman" was born.

Speaking for all good people everywhere, partisans tend to view their own ideas as the simple truth, not mere ideas. Out-group partisans have only bad ideas. Those ideas are at best wrong-headed and at worst rationalizations for darker motivations. Partisans often fail to ascribe legitimate opinions to out-groups. They view their own ideas as the simple truth, while perceiving out-group proposals as mere ploys designed to benefit themselves. To illustrate how this attitude of group superiority influences the coverage of politics, contrast the way journalists greet Republican proposals and those of the Democratic party.

When Congressional Democrats proposed a massive reorganization of the administration of health care in 1994, the press took it very seriously. The Democratic legislation was based on work done by the First Lady Hillary Rodham Clinton. Mrs. Clinton's White House Domestic Policy Council produced "A Working Group Draft" in September of 1993. The document proposed heavy government regulation of health care providers. Mrs. Clinton and her plan were treated with great respect by the Democratic Congress and the elite press. Television news aired special "public interest" programs about the Democratic medical plan. The regular evening news produced many cheerleading news reports.

Republican proposals get a very different treatment from the press. Liberal partisans in the press are ignorant of the legitimate views of Conservative Republicans, so they attribute the worst motives to them.

During the early stage of the 1996 Republican presidential primary, candidate Steve Forbes proposed a single flat rate income tax of 17 percent to replace the present graduated system. There would be no deductions. A family of four making $36,000 or less would pay nothing. The press greeted this proposal with ridicule. For instance, correspondent Eric Ingberg of the Columbia Broadcasting System (CBS) aired a "Reality Check" which characterized the flat tax as political *snake oil* and telling us that "Steve Forbes pitches his flat-tax scheme as an economic elixir, good for everything that ails us." This loaded sentence, presented as very hard news, conjures up the image of an unscrupulous con man hawking political nonsense to gullible citizens.[6] Such language is hardly non-partisan and neutral.

POLITICAL STEREOTYPING

The word *stereotype* comes to us from the printing profession. A stereotype refers to a reusable printing plate. That is, the same text could be printed over and over again. However, stereotype has come also to mean "something conforming to a fixed pattern, especially a standardized mental picture that is held in common by members of a group and that represents an oversimplified opinion." The key word is "oversimplified," because our mental pictures of the world tend to be simple when compared to reality.

Not all stereotyping is bad. Much of it is necessary. We can never get to know everything there is to know about anything. Lacking complete knowledge of people, we can only develop what amounts to a mental model. These models of people may be quite detailed or very sketchy. To one degree or other, our mental models of people are stereotypes. Most adults understand this and allow themselves the flexibility to change their minds about other people as they gain new information.

But people who build mental images with a prejudiced attitude are not apt to change their minds as they gain new information. Instead they use the new information to validate their old prejudices. Regardless of the information in hand, in-groups tend to attribute the worst characteristics of a few out-group members to the entire group.[7] Liberals tend to view Republicans as mean, unprincipled liars, who are out of touch with real people. This stereotype makes a frequent appearance on the evening news.

EXAMPLE: Insensitive Republicans

Consider this comment by journalist Sonya Friedman of the Cable News Network (CNN) from June 1991, "The perception of many Americans is that the government is now being run by a group of white middle-aged paunchy men in business suits who seem to have the interest of big business at stake. That at the expense of women, children, the poor, education, the environment and job opportunity." She is, of course, referring to Republican George Bush and his administration. Notice that she does not say who has this perception. Of course it is political Liberals who have this perception.

Remember that even bigots are not absolute in their thinking. They often allow for the possibility of exceptions to the rule. Many racial bigots have good friends from the "inferior" race. Likewise, many Liberals personally know Republicans who are decent people. However, these "good" Republicans are perceived as unusual, not the "average" Republican and definitely not leading Republicans. Sonya Friedman seems to confirm this aspect of political prejudice with the following statement: "I believe that there are Republicans who have concerns about people, humanity, education. Is it necessary that we are going to see the current decade of Republicanism mean ultra-Conservatism?"[8]

Another target of Liberal hostility is the military. Journalists, many of whom sympathized with the so-called anti-war movement of the 1960s and early seventies, have a special animus for elite military units like naval aviators and Green Berets. This 1960s mind set perceives the United States military as an instrument for evil in the world. Journalists seem to view the military establishment as an alien culture and apparently think it is their task to purify the military of its Conservative values and convert it to a Liberal institution.

Indeed, to Liberal-minded journalists, Conservative values are an abomination. Thus, Conservative leaders are stereotyped as intolerant, mean-spirited, greedy, homophobic, sexist, racist people who care only about exercising political power. Followers are stereotyped as ignorant hicks who drive around in pickups, live in "fly over country," drink name brand beer while watching mindless sports contests, and get their news from the likes of Rush Limbaugh.

POLITICAL INTOLERANCE

Most of us think we are tolerant of people with opposing points of view. We might even say it's okay to have such opinions. However, few of us truly think opposing points of view are valid or even legitimate. In fact we tend to condemn the ideas if not the person who has the offending ideas. This style of thinking is called intolerance.[9] Intolerance has deep roots. Longtime residents of a territory or region may disapprove of the strange newcomers. The people of one race, unfortunately, tend to condemn people of other races. Like other types of bigots, partisans also tend to condemn politicians with whom they strongly disagree.

Uncivil behavior is an indication of intolerance. When confronting an enemy outsider, political bigots may feel that they can dispense with the norms of civil behavior. For a display of uncivil behavior, watch news talk shows like CNN's "Cross Fire" or NBC's "MacLaughlin Group." It is not unusual for one or more of these partisans to act the intellectual bully, demanding to be heard while constantly interrupting opponents and calling them names.

EXAMPLE: Partisan Name-Calling

Another expression of intolerance is name-calling. We are all familiar with the repulsive names that racial bigots employ. Political partisans also call each other dirty names. The names fall into one or more of the following categories: 1) dirty players, 2) liars, 3) corrupt, 4) cruel and 5) racist. Exhibiting their political intolerance, the press tags Conservatives with labels like "extremist," "hate group" or "hard right." (Journalists rarely attach such labels to Liberals.) These labels say that Conservatives are not legitimate and should be roundly rejected by the public.

The Liberal press seems incapable of reporting on Republicans without calling them names like, "racist," "cynical," "insensitive," "greedy," "zealots," "liars," "obstructionists," "destructively partisan" and "bomb throwers." These dirty names are taken from actual news reports. Yes, elite journalists criticize Democrats, but journalists rarely call them names. The criticism afforded Democrats is often constructive, a kind of "tough love," if you will. The arrogant "in-your-face" type of criticism is reserved for Republicans, especially Conservatives.

Consider the comments of a few elite journalists shortly after the Los Angeles Riots of 1992. On May 3rd, *This Week With David Brinkley*, journalist Cokie Roberts commenting on the response to the riots said, "The Democratic party has failed to sufficiently condemn crime .. The Republican party has promoted racial divisions and pandered to racist attitudes." Democratic Senator Bill Bradley voiced virtually the same sentiments on the 8th of May on the *MacNeil/Lehrer News Hour*, "There has been a lack of moral leadership. Republicans used race to divide, while Democrats cloaked the self-destructive behavior of minorities in self-denial."

Journalist Roberts and Senator Bradley are voicing a political fiction common to Liberal Democrats, namely that Republicans cynically use race to divide and win elections. Notice also the false balance in these comments. They are saying that Democrats didn't quite do their job as public servants, while the Republicans are guilty of promoting racial division for political gain.

Intolerance seems to grow out of the perception that the narrow spectrum of views from one's own political grouping is the entire reach of *acceptable* opinion. Beliefs and values outside that acceptable range are viewed with mistrust. Political outsiders and their ideas may be seen as not legitimate. It is common to show disapproval of people whose ideas are considered not legitimate.

Another example of political intolerance is the press coverage of religious Conservatives. Listening to some Liberals talk about them, one might get the idea religious Conservatives are illegal political aliens with no right to participate in politics. Many suggest that religious Conservatives secretly plan to use the power of government to forcibly impose their peculiar religious values on the rest of society. That is, religious Conservatives pose a real danger to society.

The conspiracy theory that religious Conservatives are out to take over the country finds its way into the subtext of news stories. The participation in the Republican party of religious Conservatives is often described in sinister terms. If a majority of religious Conservatives get elected to some Republican state central committee, they didn't win an election, "they seized control." These "extremist religious zealots" were said to "shut out" decent Republicans from positions in the party. If a Liberal Republican loses a primary election to a religious Republican, said Liberal was "forced out." Viewers of television news are asked if "religion and politics can mix." Any participation of anyone on the "religious right" in the political process is taken as some sort of violation of the separation of church and state. This loaded imagery characterizes many news reports on religious Conservatives.

The mind set of most elite journalists views political Conservatives as alien outsiders who have no place in mass communication. For many years the news, movies and television have been Liberal territory. A few token Conservatives are allowed in, but they are often treated as outsiders with foreign habits and strange beliefs. An event which occurred at the Public Broadcasting Service (PBS) a few years back illustrates this *political xenophobia*.

EXAMPLE: Political Xenophobia at the PBS

For years after the end of the Vietnam War, Liberals in the press, in the movies and on television told the same old story of corrupt Americans defeated by virtuous peasants. This view represents the so-called "anti-war" perspective. Over the years the mass media has worked this partisan distortion into an orthodox version of that war. Unorthodox versions of the Vietnam War have been treated with xenophobic contempt.

In 1985, PBS aired a documentary series based on a book written by journalist Stanley Karnow, *Vietnam: A History*. The television series *Vietnam: A Television History* embodied the orthodox version of the war. It was produced by the PBS news magazine, *Inside Story*, in cooperation with the PBS station WGBH Boston. Political Conservatives felt that their point of view had been ignored and ridiculed by the mass media. Many in the Vietnamese community were also outraged. There were public demonstrations against PBS. Vietnamese activists called on the help of Accuracy In Media (AIM), a Conservative news watchdog group. AIM was able to force PBS to present a competing version of the history of the Vietnam War. However, PBS assigned a truth squad to neutralize it.

PBS allowed the AIM production to be aired but sought to immunize the public from these foreign Conservative ideas. Like white blood cells which surround and attack invading infections, PBS sought to weaken the public opinion potency of the information it found threatening. In media parlance, the technique is called a *wraparound*. The idea is simple. AIM would be permitted to air its program but only *inside* another PBS program. The AIM production would be surrounded with commentary which primes people to discount the AIM version of the war.

The wraparound of the AIM production, *Television's Vietnam: The Real Story*, was conducted by Mr. Arthur Miller. First there was an 18-minute setup piece which labeled the AIM production as *wrong opinion*, lest any viewer think it was being presented as *fact*. The set-up piece contained "you don't belong here" language.

The following is a sample, "Good evening, I'm Arthur Miller, the man in the middle. Tonight you are in for some unusual television. A major television organization, PBS, has agreed to let itself be criticized on its own air by *outsiders* [my emphasis] who have never produced a television program. The television organization of course is PBS. The program under fire is the much praised 13 part series *Vietnam: A Television History*. The critic is Accuracy in Media, usually known as AIM and always known as politically conservative. ... Criticism of television is so rare, the professional respect of the series so high, and Accuracy in Media so controversial, that this program, the one you are watching, has become the object of intense interest in the press." In other words, Conservatives have no business producing documentaries.

Apparently, AIM got $30,000 from the National Endowment for the Arts to help produce their documentary. PBS was outraged. Consider this from Mr. Larry Grossman who was at PBS at the time: "But in view of the rigorous efforts that the National Endowment, the other funders and PBS and everybody else went through to validate the series in the first place, to, in an offhand way, give an advocacy group with a well-known point of view, without any credentials whatsoever in the field, the opportunity to be *the* critique provider is, I think, a stunning misapplication of priorities." In other words, AIM has no business producing documentaries.

Peter McGhee, the WGBH Boston program manager stated, "I don't think it [the AIM production] meets the basic standards of credibility, journalism, what you will, that PBS customarily enforces. And they enforce against us or any other producer that comes forward with a program."

There were other voices in the set-up piece, but they were drowned out by a narration which presumed that the AIM people were untrustworthy propagandists while providing news consumers with plenty of reason to believe the PBS version was actual history. The other half of the wraparound was a discussion moderated by Miller. He continued to prime the viewers to discount the AIM production.

Arthur Miller began, "We have assembled a cast of Vietnam experts and television people to debate the merits of the AIM program we have just seen. But first, *Inside Story* has been studying the AIM program with the help of various experts both here and abroad. Here is producer Joe Russen with a report."

Mr. Russen picked up the theme, "Many people we interviewed expressed regret that AIM's critique was not sharper, more focused. There was criticism that AIM was a bit long on unprovable assertion, short on impartial assessment and ironically, burdened with annoying inaccuracies. Sometimes the problems are compounded. For example, ..." Russen took the next nineteen minutes to review and knock down what he considered the primary AIM criticism of PBS. While there were voices from both sides, Russen clearly led viewers to believe that PBS was factual and AIM was not.

In the 20-minute discussion that followed, PBS stacked the deck against AIM. Of the six participants, three of them were PBS higher-ups. The remaining three were essentially neutral during the discussion. The moderator allowed the pro-PBS people to verbally attack the sole AIM person, Mr. Reed Irvine, without giving him adequate time to respond. The moderator Mr. Miller also attacked Irvine. "Mr. Irvine, did you think you were producing a documentary?"

Irvine responded that he was producing a criticism. "Wait, wait. It seems to me that you are projecting your opinion."

Thus the AIM production was not a documentary or even legitimate criticism. At best it was "viewer response" presented by a group of outsiders who just wanted to get their propaganda message aired. The audience was indirectly told over and over again not to confuse the AIM production with truth-telling PBS documentaries.

Miller ended with the following, "Gentlemen, we end as we began, in controversy. Tonight we've gone Shakespeare's Hamlet one better than a play within a play. What we have done is a program about a program about a program about a program. But despite the obvious complications, we think there are two distinct pluses from all of this. The first is to allow conflicting views about the Vietnam War to be presented at a time, when the nation as a whole, is allowing itself a close look at the only war we have ever lost. The other plus was permitting network time to take issue with a presentation by the same network. That's a beginning at least that we hope will broaden debate and allow viewers to talk back to an impersonal presence in their lives. When it was designed and licensed, television was supposed to allow for all sides of an issue to be heard in the public interest. We hope you have found this effort to be, at least, be a small step in that direction."

It was a very small step indeed. It is certainly in the right direction, in my opinion. However, in the years since this program was aired, I have seen no further steps.

If PBS routinely presented "controversial" documentaries with this same type of critical wraparound, the treatment of AIM would only be unfair and unbalanced. What makes the PBS response to AIM xenophobic is the double standard, one for outsiders, another for insiders. Only AIM, with its foreign beliefs has gotten this aggressive truth squad wraparound. PBS documentaries with a Liberal bent don't get this sort of nasty treatment.

Indeed, the unencumbered airing of documentaries embracing Liberal opinion is routine at PBS. The Center for Media and Public Affairs performed content analysis study of all the of PBS documentaries aired in the year 1987. From the conclusion, " ... there can be little doubt that the ideas expressed on public affairs issues were far more consonant with the beliefs and preferences of contemporary American liberals than with those of conservatives."[10]

The conclusion went on to state, "In short, on the social and political controversies addressed by PBS documentaries across a full year of programs, the balance of opinion tilted consistently in a liberal direction.

If these public broadcasting documentaries fell short of the standard of diversity by failing to give voice to *excluded groups*, [emphasis added] they also fell short of the standard of balance by failing to present both sides on issues that produce partisan cleavages on the current political spectrum."

KEY CONCEPT

I'm not saying every Liberal minded-journalist is dedicated to his prejudices all of the time. Some journalists are obvious steadfast partisans, while others perceive their own biases and take real steps to control them. I'm not saying that every news story is crudely laced with Liberal bias. If this were the case, the press would lose all credibility. I'm not saying that all media bias is Liberal. There is a small, feisty Conservative bias in the news.

I am, however, saying that prejudices common to political Liberals find a happy home in elite newsrooms. I am saying that enough journalists allow their political prejudices to influence their work to excessively distort the images of news events. I am saying that the social psychology of prejudice explains much of the political bias seen in the news media and partisan passions explain most of the rest. I am saying that political prejudice distorts the content of the news.

The notion of prejudice and bigotry is based the assumption that the social demographics of all groups of sufficient size is roughly the same. That is, no group has a monopoly on truth, smarts, stupidity, virtue or sin. I assume that the social psychology of prejudice applies equally to all groups: New Yorkers, southerners, Germans, Chinese, academics, farmers, Republicans, Democrats and journalists.

I assume that we live in a politically pluralistic society which breaks down into Liberal, Conservative, Libertarian, Populist and Drop-outs in roughly even divisions of about twenty percent each. Each of these groups represents a major style of thinking about society and government. I assume that each group has the truth in about the same proportion as the other groups. None is more or less virtuous than the other. None is more or less sinful that the other.

I assume that news organizations confront their own political prejudices just like other organizations have confronted their own racial or gender prejudices. First, journalists claim that they are not biased. Then they engage in tokenism as discriminatory practices became more subtle. Then journalists will claim that the bias they denied has been removed from the news. In other words, real change in the way the journalism establishment does business will be slow and grudging.

DISCUSSION

In this chapter I drew on ideas from the psychology of racial prejudice and sought to apply those ideas to political prejudice. To begin with, I sought a good definition of *prejudice*. The dictionary told me prejudice was prejudging. Academics favored a definition in terms of *racial* prejudice. The most general definition I could find was provided by Professor Douglas W. Bethlehem of Leeds University in Great Britian. He defined prejudice as, "An opinion or belief held by anyone on any subject which in the absence of or in contradiction to, adequate test or logically derived conclusion or comparison with objective reality, is maintained as fact by the person espousing it, and may be acted on though it were demonstrably true." In other words, prejudging. I adopted and adapted this definition.

It is when people obstinately cling to their offensive prejudices in the face of overwhelmingly evidence to the contrary, that we normally use the word "prejudice." This usage of the word "prejudice" is what the dictionary calls "bigotry." While I make a distinction between "prejudice" and "bigotry," many people do not.

Strictly speaking, it isn't possible to think without prejudice. Bias is an unavoidable aspect of the human condition. We rarely have complete information about anything. We are often forced to decide and act on something with less than adequate evidence. So we constantly act on beliefs as if they were fact. To do otherwise would overload our cognitive processing. I call this natural cognitive prejudice. This form of prejudice is not what we ordinarily think of as prejudice, however. The idea of using a broad definition is to show that treating beliefs as proven fact (that is, prejudice) is an unavoidable aspect of our thinking process.

Prejudice is a tar baby. People who fight prejudice often trade one form of bigotry for another. People fighting *racial* bigotry may become *political* bigots. And too often the target of prejudice returns bigotry for bigotry. You can't fight prejudice by simply coming out against it. I don't have much faith in the utility of so-called "sensitivity training." The act of forcing sensitivity on somebody else is really another form of bigotry. Such authoritarian solutions to the problem of offensive prejudice fail to teach subjects that undisciplined thinking is the problem.

I focus on the political prejudice of political Liberals because they dominate elite news organizations. However, it is important to observe that no group, political or otherwise, is free of bias. The analysis presented in this book applies equally to the tiny Conservative press which includes, Fox News, The Christian Broadcasting System, some of talk radio and *The Washington Times*. When Conservatives come to dominate news organizations, Hollywood movies and television programming, as Liberals do now, I will be happy to write a book critical of bias in a Conservative media. Until that day I will continue to report on the *Liberal* press.

END NOTES

(1) I use a nonstandard convention for capitalizing the names of political parties. For instance, I capitalize "Democratic Party" to signify that the phrase is a noun, not an adjective describing the nature of the political party. The object here is to eliminate any confusion between the group of people identified as "Democrats" and the widely held *democratic* ideals common to many political organizations in western societies. I make the same distinction between the group of people known as the "Republican Party" and republican ideals common to many political organizations.

I also use a nonstandard convention for capitalizing the names of political philosophies. I capitalize both the political activity of people and their apparent philosophy. For instance the word "Liberal" with a capital "L" refers to the partisan activities as well as the political attitudes of certain people like Senator Edward Kennedy, President William Clinton and PBS media mogul Bill Moyers. I use the word "Liberal" to refer to the cultural attitudes of the wider Liberal community. However, a small "l" liberal refers to the usual dictionary definition, that is, a person who is non-orthodox and characteristically generous and broad-minded. Likewise, the word "Conservative" with a capital "C" refers to the political attitude typified by former President Ronald Reagan, PBS commentator William F. Buckley Jr. and Senator Jesse Helms as well as the cultural attitudes of the community of people who identify themselves as Conservatives. The word conservative with a small "c" refers to the usual dictionary definition, that is, one who adheres to traditional ways of thinking and doing things.

(2) Of course, one would find an intolerance of things Liberal, if Conservatives dominated the prestige press. But since that is not the case, I will concentrate on the Liberal prejudices.

(3) An in-group is the group to which a person belongs. An out-group is a group to which a person does not belong. The terms "in-group" and "out-group" are designed to accentuate contrasting perspectives between members of various groups. These terms are used when there is some general principle that can be applied to the perceptions of all members of all groups. For instance, both Republicans and Democrats think their policies are superior to those of the other party. Thus it can be said that in-group partisans view their own polices as superior.

(4) Professor Douglas W. Bethlehem in his book, **A Social Psychology of Prejudice**, defines ethnocentrism "as a tendency to glorify the in-group while denigrating out-groups." If the definition is taken quite literally, it can apply to any group, New Yorkers, grocers, Europeans, members of a private club, as well as political groups like Conservative Republicans, the religious right, the religious left, Liberal Democrats, the National Rifle Association and National Organization for Women.

(5) In its worst form, this attitude of moral superiority is used to justify doing horrendous things to out-group people. In this century, Nazi death camps in Europe and Communist death camps in the former Soviet Union and other parts of the world are examples of moral superiority carried to extreme. The Spanish Inquisition and the excesses of the French Revolution are also good examples of the evils of cultural-centrism.

(6) CBS's "Reality Check" is a regular news segment which purports to compare *reality* to a popular perception, the statements of public figures, etc. Mr. Eric Engberg has been the usual correspondent for the "Reality Check."

The reality check on candidate Forbes was so biased that fellow CBS journalist Bernard Goldberg wrote an opinion piece that ran in the *Wall Street Journal* of February 13, 1996. Mr. Goldberg analyzes a reality check done by Engberg. According to Mr. Goldberg, Engberg "set new standards for bias." I agree.

Snake oil was an inert substance sold to gullible patrons of carnival sideshows in the nineteenth and early twentieth centuries as active medicine. Salesmen would claim "marvelous restorative powers" of their elixir. Thus Engberg's reference to an elixir is a clear reference to this sleazy business practice of an earlier time. Snake oil becomes a name for any sort of foolishness packaged by a con man to appear authentic. See page 535 of the **Morris Dictionary of Word and Phrase Origins** by William and Mary Morris, second edition, published by Harper and Row in 1988.

(7) I believe that all the major political groups -- Liberals, Conservatives, Libertarians and Populists -- are mostly populated by good people trying to do the right thing as they see it. Each group, however, has its share of nuts, extremists and nogoodniks. In other words, I think that an unbiased statistical sample of Republicans and Democrats would show a spectrum of good people with a few bad apples. Each party would have its share of crooks. See also "Key Concepts" at the end of the chapter.

(8) This discussion took place right after Judge Thomas was nominated to the Supreme Court in June 1991. Sonya Friedman of CNN was discussing current political issues with David Gergen (then affiliated with U.S. News and World Report) and William Schneider who is still a political analyst for CNN. Gergen referred to the stereotype that a Republican is someone who does not care.

(9) See page 4 of, **A Social Psychology of Prejudice**, by Douglas W. Bethlehem, published in 1985 by Croom Helm Ltd, in England. Even though the idea of *intolerance* is conceptually very different

than the idea of *prejudice*, it may very well be that bigots tend to be intolerant as well as prejudiced.

(10) See the conclusion of the study *Balance and Diversity in PBS Documentaries* by S. Robert Lichter, Daniel Amundson and Linda S. Lichter of the Center for Media And Public Affairs, 2101 L Street, N.W. Suite 405, Washington, D.C. 20037 dated March 1992.

Chapter 2

PERCEPTION BIAS

Are they "the homeless" or just plain "bums?" In most of our cities and towns are people of meager means who live in streets and alleys. They have been referred to as street people. When viewing such a scene, one person, Ms. Barbara Bleeding-Hart, perceives unfortunate "homeless" people. Another person, Mr. Harry Hardnose, perceives "bums" who have given up on life. This conflict in perception defines a major fault line in political thinking.

A long-time political activist, the compassionate Barbara Bleeding-Hart has worked very hard to help those she considers less fortunate. She perceives the homeless as the necessary consequence of a heartless capitalism. Listening to Barbara, you would get the idea that there are legions of homeless posing a social emergency that requires a massive new federal program. Barbara believes in a style of Liberalism that requires a powerful central government to do good in the world. The stereotype of the oppressed poor is very real to Ms. Hart. She actually perceives homelessness when she sees street people.

Harry Hardnose, the local manager of Coldwater Bank, is Barbara's ideological opposite. Harry is a true believer in an authoritarian style of capitalism that admits only a chosen elite into its ranks. Hardnose does not take kindly to any talk to the contrary. Harry is fond of talking about the "tough business decisions" he has made. That means he cheats his employees on their paychecks. If you listen to him, you would get the idea that there are only two kinds of ordinary people, those with a job and those who are lazy. He takes it as given that anyone who is not working is a "bum." The *bum* stereotype is very real to Harry. He really *sees* "bums" when he looks at street people.

Harry Hardnose does not think he has any political beliefs about street people. As Harry sees it, there is nothing political; it's the simple truth. However, he does think that Barbara gets all ideological about her homeless folk. Barbara is just as closed-minded of course. She thinks her perception of the homeless is the simple truth. And she thinks that Harry is driven by his heartless Conservative ideology. How do Harry and Barbara come up with such conflicting perceptions of the same people? Let's start with Barbara.

How did Barbara see the homeless? The first thing to understand is that, **seeing is a thinking task**. People must think in order to see. This is true even for mundane perceptions. For instance, it is Barbara's knowledge of cats that allows her to see a cat. But there can be problems even with simple perceptions. When a friend shows her a pet echidna, Barbara does not recognize it, and she asks, "What's that?" She does not know what she is looking at. She had no knowledge of this animal. She see's an animal but is not able to see a spiny anteater. In order to see anything, Barbara has to evaluate the present and remember the past. Let's take a look at how her memory of the past helps her to see the homeless of the present.

Barbara has two memory centers, short term and long term. Her short-term memory is what she pays attention to at any moment. Short-term memory contains new information Barbara just received with her eyes and ears. Short-term memory also contains information she retrieved from her long-term memory. However, short-term memory is limited. Barbara can pay attention to only a small number of things at one time. As she perceives a street person, she remembers the street person who told her all about his recent streak of bad luck. She remembers parts of an hour-long news special highlighting the underside of capitalism. These retrieved memories color her perceptions of current events.

Like the rest of us, Barbara's long-term memory contains a lifetime of past memories. Barbara stores that information in various categories. (Exactly how that is done is apparently not well known.) For instance, she has categories for cats, houses, cars, Liberals, Conservatives, incompetent dolts, a federal program, global warming and gun control. Other categories contain knowledge about individuals and groups of individuals. She also has categories containing scenarios of how life events typically occur. Memory information in these categories can be specific or abstract, spotty or extensive, simplistic or complex. Her long-term memory contains "the information we typically think of as world knowledge."[1]

Barbara's world knowledge includes her ideas about the homeless and other beliefs. Ideas about the way the world works are a very important group of categories. *Beliefs figure strongly in how Barbara stores and retrieves information in her long-term memory.* Before Barbara lays her eyes on a street person, she already has a mental category of the homeless in her long-term memory. She also has the idea that a cruel, selfish capitalism causes good people to become the homeless.

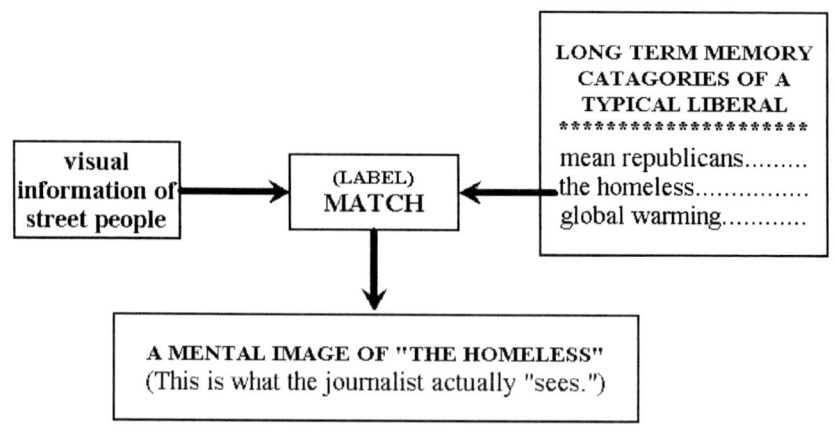

COGNITIVE MATCHING

When Barbara "sees" a homeless person, she is matching her visual information of the street people before her eyes to her long term memory category of stored information about the homeless. The experience is totally real to her. Using her beliefs about street people, she constructs a mental image of homeless. However, she is not aware of the construction. She does not understand that believing is required in order for her to see the homeless. She takes her beliefs to be reality. She does not understand that *believing is seeing.*

Harry Hardnose goes through a similar process to create his reality of "bums." Harry does not have a mental category of homeless so he does not see them. However, he has a well-developed category of "bums" with lots of information that is consistent with his political prejudices. Like Barbara, Harry uses that memory information to recognize street people as "bums." Like Barbara, he thinks his perceptions are unbiased. Journalists also fall prey to the same prejudiced style of thinking. Journalists also think they are unbiased.

Journalists claim that they can produce the news without significant bias. However, evidence from the field of psychology suggests that journalists don't set their political preferences aside. Such evidence suggests that journalistic opinion distorts the perception of leading journalists which in turn distorts the various mental tasks they perform.

An important mental task is categorizing people and events. Categorizing involves the cognitive matching described above. This shapes the whole direction of the news. A journalist categorizing street people as "bums" will write one kind of story; a journalist categorizing street people as homeless will write an entirely different story. Categorizing influences every other mental task. Relying on the homeless category, journalists *infer* a reality of homeless people as victims of a "hands-off Daddy Warbucks" capitalism. All their other mental tasks fall in line with the original assessment.

Explaining current events is an important mental task. But the inferences already made severely limit the list of allowable explanations. If a street person allegedly commits a crime, journalists will explain that it was heartless capitalism that made him homeless in the first place. When journalists question city officials, they go after the homeless story, not the story about criminals. When journalists encounter unwanted information suggesting that the homeless version of events is not true, they easily find some way to dispose of it. Finally, journalists must produce something people can read in a newspaper or view on television. Two important tasks are involved here. Journalists *select and integrate* information into narrative stories suitable for various news products.[2] The narrative story will, of course, conform to the homeless victim theme.

As shown in Chapter 3, Liberal prejudices dominate the entire press establishment to the virtual exclusion of other points of view. This means that Liberal memory categories influence the mental tasks performed by the vast majority of working journalists. In other words, Liberal prejudices distort the thinking of leading journalists. And it is journalists who bring us the news.

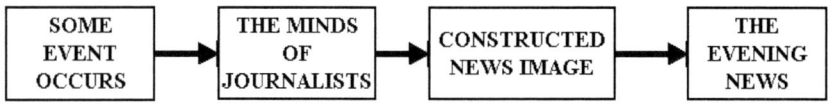

For news to get from some remote event to our living room television, it must pass through the minds of journalists. As the news makes that trip, it gets filtered by the Liberal prejudices of leading journalists. Thus, what we "see" on the evening news is not the actual events of the day, but a Liberal version of those events. Media bias becomes more than a superficial tilt to the Liberal side of the political equation. Liberal prejudices are the heart and soul of the practice of today's journalism. The distortion of current events begins with the mental task of categorizing. An automatic consequence of categorizing is labeling.

LOADED LABELS

As we have seen with Barbara and Harry, labels are no mere grammatical necessity. Labeling is integral to perception. And journalists are paid to perceive events and tell us all about it. When a journalist perceives a car, for instance, he matches the object in his vision to his knowledge about cars, automatically attaching the label "car." Attaching labels to physical objects involves little dispute. It is when journalists get to labeling more abstract objects, that their political opinions contaminate what they think they "see."

The perceptions of politically partisan journalists are susceptible to distortion. Labels loaded with Liberal prejudices pop into the minds of elite journalists as revealed truth. Consider the way journalists have labeled the decade of the 1980s. As already noted, Democrats and elite journalists perceive the 1980s as a dark age because Republican Ronald Reagan was President. The following diagram illustrates how journalists perceive this "Decade of Greed" prejudice as proven fact.

When presented with information about the 1980s, the first thing a journalist does is to categorize it. Journalists will match that information with their memory category "Decade of Greed." Since categorizing is integral to perception itself, the label "Decade of Greed" is automatic.[3] They will go on to retrieve memories from that category to explain information about the 1980s. The loaded label attached to the explanation is then stored in long-term memory, to be retrieved later. Journalists will remember their explanation of the 1980s, rather than the raw data. Present a Liberal-minded journalist with information which suggests that a lot of good things happened in the 1980s and he will resist matching that information with his good times. Thus, he will have a difficult time perceiving the 1980s as anything but a "decade of greed." The undisciplined mind often falls prey to a self-fulfilling prophecy.

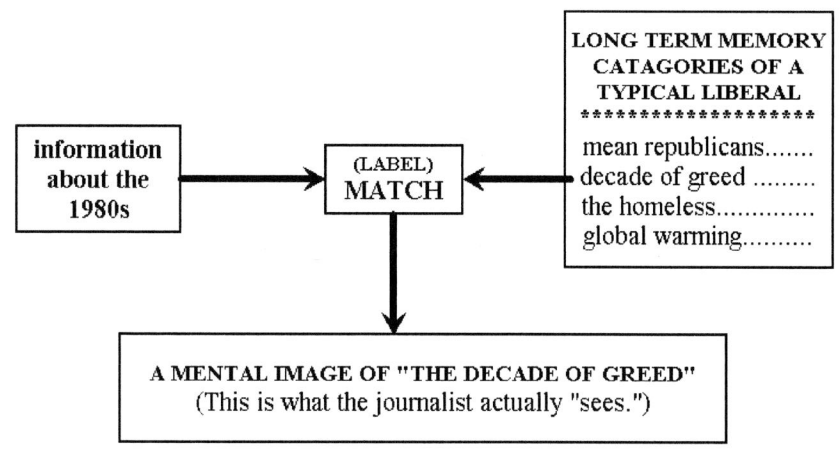

COGNITIVE CATEGORIZING

The coverage of the dispute over a woman's right to an abortion provides a good example of *ideologically* loaded labels. In the dispute there is a liberal side and a conservative side. Liberals perceive the fetus to be blob of non-sentient flesh. From the legal point of view, Liberals define a citizen as a born person. Thus, the unborn fetus is a thing, not a person. Given this view, the decision on whether to kill a thing (the fetus) logically rests solely with the mother. It is, therefore, her choice. They logically perceive anyone who opposes them as trying to take an important right (to choose) away from women.

However, Conservatives perceive the fetus to be an unborn child, with full citizenship rights. Since the mother has no right to kill her children, she has no fundamental right to abortion. Conservatives take the position that unborn children have a fundamental right to life. As they strive to save the lives of unborn children, they logically perceive anyone who opposes them as favoring the killing of unborn children.

In my view, the abortion issue is a classic case of citizens claiming conflicting rights. Each side presents itself as the protector of democratic rights. Each side favors rights. Liberals favor the right of the mother to have complete control over her own body, including her fetus. This gives her the right to remove the fetus from her body as she might remove her appendix. Conservatives confer citizenship on the fetus, thus giving the fetus the right to live. However, each side is also against rights. Conservatives are against the right of the mother to kill the fetus. Liberals are against the right of the fetus to live.

While journalists don't usually overtly express pro-abortion opinions, they do use a set of labels common to the pro-abortion side of the issue. Journalists opt for the labels, "abortion rights" versus "anti-abortionists." Taken together these two labels imply that the pro-life side is against the rights of women. This pair of labels is unbalanced and unfair. To illustrate the unfairness, consider the labels a Conservative Press might use: "pro-life" versus "pro-abortionist," or "anti-abortion versus "anti-life."

What is the remedy? Journalists could call activist groups what they want to be called. The press could use the labels *"pro-life"* and *"pro-choice,"* which is what Conservatives and Liberals call themselves, respectively. I favor the labels "fetus rights" versus "abortion rights." These labels state the legal issue without siding with one side or the other.

Coverage of the Cold War provided more examples of ideologically loaded labels. Most Liberals perceived a political landscape with left wing Communists at one extreme opposed by right wing Conservatives at the other end. The more radical Liberals felt that Communism held out a great hope for mankind. These Liberals eagerly rushed to the defense of Communists when they were under attack by Conservatives during the Cold War. However, most Liberals considered American Conservatives the real danger to freedom during the Cold War.

During the Cold War, Republican President Ronald Reagan labeled communist Russia "the evil empire," and the press jeered him. But when Russian Communism collapsed, KGB files revealed that there was indeed an "evil empire." Liberal-minded journalists could no longer deny that Communists were *bad guys*. Landing on their lexical feet, they invented the incredible label, "conservative Communists." The logic may have worked like this. From the Liberal point of view, Conservatives are the bad guys. If Communists are bad, they must be conservative Communists! Or the usage of the word "conservative" may be justified by claiming that the reference is to small "c" conservatives who want to maintain the status quo. Even if the latter were the case, journalists were still quite willing to allow news consumers to confuse small "c" conservatives in the Communist party with capital "C" Conservatives in the Republican party.

CONNECTING THE DOTS

Journalists claim to simply report what they "see;" and that's our problem. They do report what they "see." Journalists "see" *homeless* on the streets. Journalists "saw" an intolerant Republican convention in August of 1992. Journalists "saw" principled Democrats opposing Republican Presidents. Journalists continue to "see" mean-spirited Republicans on the campaign trail. Journalists "saw" a "decade of greed" in the 1980s. Journalists "saw" *Conservative Communists* with the collapse of the Soviet Union. During The Cold War, journalists failed to "see" a serious Communist threat to the United States. In 1992, journalists failed to "see" a good economy until after Democrat William Clinton was elected.

We don't "see" only with our eyes; we also "see" with our minds. Perceptions are a mental construct. Perception of physical objects is fairly concrete. We might perceive a physical object to be a Ford station wagon, but the object turns out to be a Toyota. However, we never perceive a Ford station wagon that turns out to be a World War Two bomber. The abstract portion of perceiving physical objects like cars is small. Perceptions vary little from person to person.

Perceiving abstract economic events is a whole different matter. There is a concrete aspect to evaluating an economy to be sure. Measures include growth rate, stock market average, savings rate and percentage of people unemployed. Perception of economic events is a mental construct resulting from evaluating such economic data. Unlike the perceptions of concrete objects like cars, there can be wide disagreement among competent people over the more abstract economic events.

Some abstract events turn out to be quite real, while others never occur. Journalists perceive abstract events with their minds, not their eyes. Thus perceptions will be only as good as their thinking. A trained, disciplined journalist can discern abstract events that can actually happen. Unfortunately most elite journalists are sloppy-thinking political partisans who see events that don't happen. That's exactly what occurred during the presidential campaign of 1992.

Remember that Republican George Bush was President. The partisan prejudices of the elite press motivated them to experience a dark age. Like their fellow Democrats working for the election of William Clinton, journalists were motivated to perceive an economy in recession. (If voters thought the economy was good, they might vote for Republican President George Bush.) The press reported that the economy was in recession. But in November, 1992, Clinton defeated Bush. The press was no longer motivated to perceive a recession. Thus, a recovered economy miraculously appeared on the evening news, just days after the 1992 election. How were journalists able to perceive a recession, when the economy was in recovery?

In short, journalists yielded to their partisan passions and jumped to conclusions. Journalists carefully selected some actual economic information and fleshed out a mental picture with memory information of a bad economy. The result was a perception of an economy in recession. They took the resulting economic fiction, loaded with its anti-Republican prejudices, to be reality. Journalists based their economic reporting on this "reality." During the 1992 election, the elite press told voters that the economy was in recession. But with the election of Democrat William Clinton, the media elite allowed themselves to perceive an economy in recovery. The reality of the 1992 recession persists to this day. As late as November 1996 journalists were still ridiculing President George Bush for failing to perceive the alleged recession in 1992. See the chart on page 29.

The 1992 recession was created by transforming real events into a fictional event. Other fictional events are constructed by falsely connecting real events. Constructing links between events is basic to understanding the world. Linking events is a natural and necessary practice. However, people often impose a relationship between events where none exists. It is called an *illusory correlation*.[4] It makes sense that journalists would also make false correlations. The fact that 80 to 90 percent of journalists vote for the Democratic candidate for President suggests the political direction of their false correlations. Indeed. My study of the press suggests that journalists go beyond the facts in an effort to link Republicans to bad things.

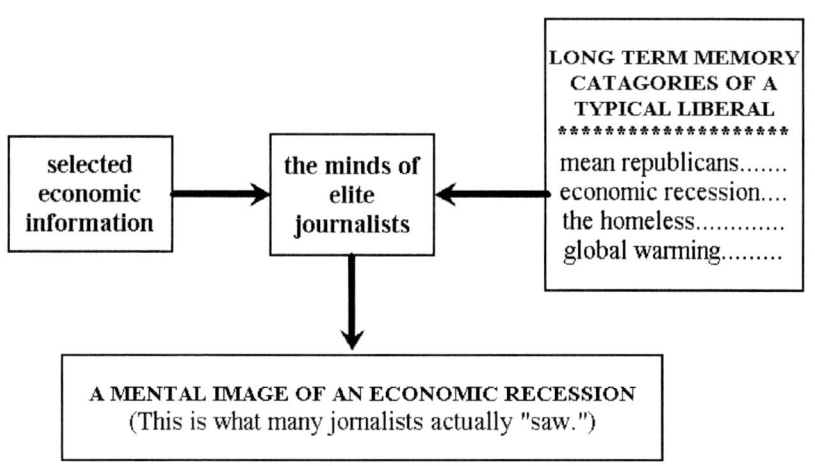

CONSTRUCTING AN ECONOMIC FICTION

The elite press requires no evidence at all to link leading Republicans to wrongdoing, only a strong *suspicion*. It might be done by overt statement. It might be done indirectly. It might be suggested rather than stated outright. However it's done, the *false link* is made. A good example of false linkage was the press coverage of an event that was supposed to have happened in the fall of 1980, the so-called October Surprise.

EXAMPLE: The October Surprise

On August 5, 1991, just a few months before the beginning of the 1992 presidential campaign, correspondent Roger Mudd of PBS's "MacNeil/Lehrer News Hour" explained the accusations this way, "Exactly five minutes after President Reagan took the oath of office in January 1981, Iran released the 52 American hostages it had held in Tehran for 444 days. In the week following the inauguration, the international media exploded with pictures of the hostages and their jubilant families. At the same time a large shipment of arms was secretly sent to Iran, by way of Israel, in spite of an American arms embargo. *The timing of these two events eventually lead to the suspicion of a secret arms for hostage deal* [Emphasis added]. The charge, that top Reagan campaign officials made a secret deal with Iran to delay the hostages' release, so that President Carter would not get any last minute boost before the November election. The hostage crisis had dominated the 1980 campaign year. ... "

Notice that the release of the hostages and the inauguration of Republican Reagan were linked simply because there were five minutes between the events. What else must journalists believe to be true for them to be so ready to jump to such a conclusion? Look at the accusation. It embodied the partisan attitude that Democrats have towards leading successful Republicans. The Republican camp was accused of deliberately extending the captivity of the 52 American hostages in a contemptible trick to gain political advantage in the 1980 election. The readiness of journalists to believe such obviously partisan accusations suggests that they already believed that Republicans were uncaring, selfish people who would do anything to gain power.

In 1991, Reagan was out of office and Republican George Bush was president. The attack on Bush began on April 15, 1991, with a *New York Times* article written by Mr. Gary Sick, a former aide to President James Carter. The next day the PBS news show "Frontline" aired a one-hour expose style report entitled, "The Election Held Hostage." For the next eight months the press had a field day. The television networks jumped on the story, airing 27 news pieces between April 15 and December 31, 1991. ABC "Nightline" ran its own expose.

And Gary Sick published his attack book, *October Surprise: America's Hostages in Iran and the Election of Ronald Reagan.* The press jumped to the conclusion that the accusation was certainly viable, if not yet proven. There was always the sense in news stories that the proof was about to surface. Thus, the elite press gave this obvious partisan attack a long friendly hearing. The dominant message of the coverage was that President Bush was exactly the kind of person who would do such bad things.

If proven true, the so-called October Surprise would surely have turned public opinion against the Republicans. It is likely that President Bush would have been impeached or driven from office. The prospect of bringing down another Republican President energized the press coverage. If the opportunity presented itself, the press surely would have fanned the partisan accusation into a firestorm of negative public opinion that would have driven President Bush from office.

But it was not to be. The Liberal opinion magazine *New Republic*, to its credit, blew the whistle on the story in a November 18, 1991 issue. And on January 13, 1993, a bipartisan House of Representatives task force, which had been investigating the allegations, released its final report. The Reagan campaign was completely exonerated. The House investigation administered the coup de grace to the October Surprise story. It turned out there was little evidence, save the wishful thinking of disappointed Democrats and elite journalists.

Predictably the Congressional report got little play in the press. What got even less exposure, was the discovery, by the Congress, that President James Carter had offered Iran $150 million in spare parts and $80 million in cash for the return of the 52 hostages! Evidently the Democrats were working on their own October surprise.[5] While enthusiastic to go with a story in a way that would cause maximum damage to Republicans, the elite press is very reluctant to give Democrats the same treatment.

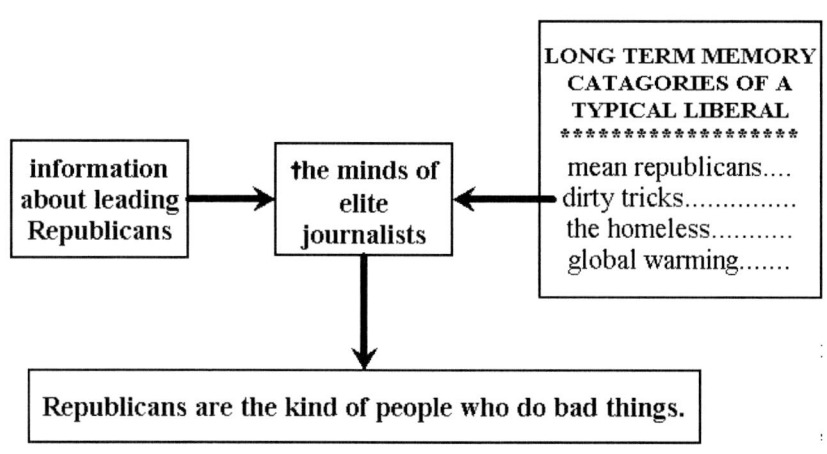

CONSTRUCTING A FALSE LINKAGE

There was not a shred of truth in the October Surprise story, yet journalists eagerly went beyond any facts to perceive heartless Republicans willing to do anything to win the Presidency including leaving 52 Americans imprisoned in Iran until after the election. If journalists did not perceive the October Surprise as actual, proven fact, the coverage certainly suggested that it was a likely possibility.

With the aid of their own political prejudices, journalists linked Republicans to a dirty campaign trick, the so-called October Surprise. Only mentally undisciplined journalists would be so eager to believe so much on so little evidence. Even though this particular dirty trick turned out to be totally untrue, news consumers were still told that Republicans are dirty players. Voters were still told to disapprove of Republicans.

Journalists have a whole different attitude toward Democrats. When judging Democrats, journalists adopt a very strict standard. Journalists are very reluctant to go beyond the facts and connect Democrats to anything bad. Journalists may fail to see causal connections where they likely exist. When scandal information surfaces right next to a leading Democrat, journalists are loath to make the obvious connection. The Whitewater Scandal coverage provides numerous examples.

EXAMPLE: The Missing Whitewater Link

On May 28, 1996 the former business partners of President Clinton, James and Susan McDougal, were convicted in Little Rock, Arkansas court of fraud and conspiracy. The sitting governor of Arkansas, Democrat Jim Guy Tucker, also was convicted. Democrat Clinton had testified in a video deposition to the innocence of these now convicted felons.[6] Certainly common sense implies that there is a link. For any Republican President, the video would have been more than enough for journalists to make the causal link. However, Democrats are treated differently.

In news stories about the Whitewater convictions, the press refused to suggest that there might be a connection to President Clinton. In fact, journalists usually leaped to the defense of the President. They typically reminded news consumers that President Clinton had not been accused of any crime by any official judicial branch of government. This linguistic maneuver implies that the President was in the clear and people should continue to approve of him. The common sense standard is just not good enough to link a leading Democrat to anything bad.

Journalists needed very hard proof, the proverbial smoking gun, to connect President Clinton to his former business partners. Being in business with people who later were proven to be criminals is not enough evidence to even suggest that Democratic President Clinton might be linked to any wrongdoing. This legalistic *smoking gun standard* is appropriate for the courtroom, not the newsroom. Apparently the Washington press corps needs indisputable proof that President Clinton had committed a serious felony while in the office of the presidency in order to make the link. Contrast these news judgements with those made during the coverage of the so-called October surprise.

Research from psychology shows that people go "beyond the given data, fleshing out the skeletal picture, with information from the stored category representation." [7] Conservatives go beyond the data to flesh out a Conservative reality. Liberals go beyond the facts to flesh out a Liberal version of reality. Since the press is dominated by political Liberals, that's the version of reality we see on the evening news. Journalists create that reality by the way they gather and organize information.

HANDLING RAW NEWS INFORMATION

It is one of those facts of life that information about any event is typically incomplete and confusing. Journalists can only gather bits and pieces of information about any news event. Often the precise piece of information needed to draw a definite conclusion is annoyingly absent. Since information is always incomplete, a journalist will never have enough information to prove a story true in an absolute sense. Thus he can always claim to be short of information and be telling the truth. On the other hand, a journalist can always go with a story with slim supporting evidence, claiming that no journalism would be done if a high standard of proof is required. In this case, he would also be telling the truth.

Since they are always "telling a truth," journalists have the confidence to routinely ignore the facts or go beyond the facts as they promote their political prejudices as political reality. Deciding when to connect the dots is key to maintaining unproven prejudices as proven fact. Thus journalists selectively validate the truth and relevance of raw information.

Of course, we all do it. The incomplete nature of raw information and our faulty capacity to understand it requires all of us to employ our prejudices. It's unavoidable. **We have to selectively handle information in order to maintain any sense of reality.** Different people maintain different realities.

In America, there are roughly four political realities: Liberal, Conservative, Libertarian and Populist. Likely, each of these realities represents some of part of the truth. And each of these realities employs fiction. The problem is that the elite media does not give each reality a fair hearing. In fact, elite journalists promote the Liberal version as "the objective reality."

Before journalists present news information to the public, they are supposed to make sure they have their facts right. Confirming a news story requires a reality check of some sort. But in the political monoculture of elite news rooms, fact checking is a circular process. When a journalists tests his Liberal version of events against his Liberal sense of reality, he confirms the Liberal version of events as true. It's the cognitive fox guarding the information henhouse.

Some research bears this out. Consider how journalists handle partisan news sources. According to the book, *The Media Elite*, journalists regard information supplied by political Liberals as more reliable than information from political Conservative groups.[8] The range of sources becomes restricted so that the Liberal version of the story appears to be the only logical option. Conservatives are apt to supply information that Liberal-minded journalists don't want to hear. Liberal sources confirm the Liberal reality that dominates elite newsrooms.

Journalists, like other people, have a strong tendency to devise testing strategies that will automatically confirm their version of events. Consciously or subconsciously, *journalists tend to select* information for serious consideration which confirms their version of events while, at the same time, finding a way to avoid *serious* consideration of disconfirming information. This tendency is known as *selective perception.*[9]

Selective perception is a universal tendency. When presented with information that supports the desired point of view, people accept it as true and store it in long-term memory. But when confronted with unwanted information that threatens a beloved belief, people will explain it away. People may regard the unwanted information as 1) unreliable or arising from shoddy sources, 2) transient or situationally induced, or 3) superficial or not important. Liberal-minded journalists are also people, so they have the same tendency.

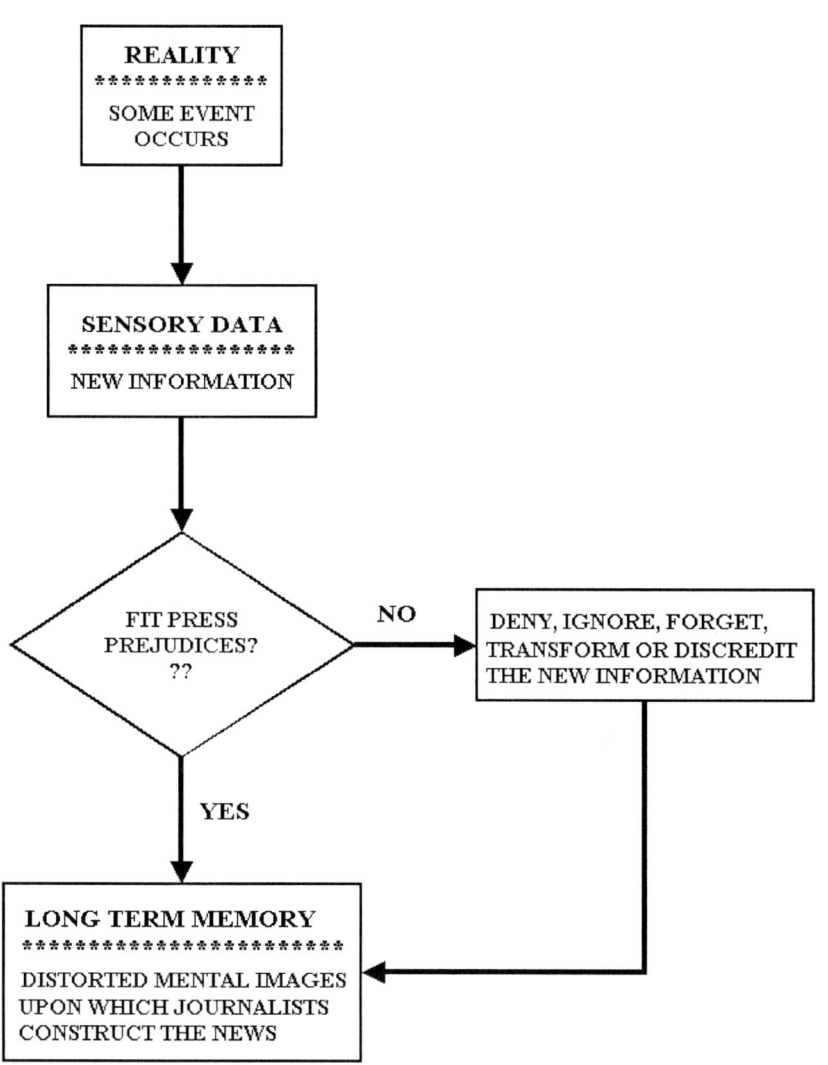

SELECTIVE PERCEPTION

Some newsworthy event occurs. The event may contain information that confirms a journalist's prejudices or it may not. The important point is that it does not matter. If the event contains information that confirms his Liberal prejudices, that information is presented to the public as proven fact. If the news event contains information that runs counter to his Liberal prejudices, he has trouble "seeing" it. This aspect of the story may have trouble becoming news. And if it does make the news, journalists will question its veracity.

Selective perception explains how journalists are able to maintain their Liberal prejudices regardless of the amount or high quality of disconfirming information that they may encounter. Selective perception is a kind of filter that helps them maintain their prejudices. Thus the evening news always has a Liberal glow to it.

A common reaction is to simply deny that the bad news is even true. Psychologists call this response *denial*. A good example of denial was seen in the response of some Liberals to an acid rain study conducted in the 1980s at the behest of the federal government. For some time before that, many Liberals believed that man-made acid rain was destroying the forests and lakes of the northeastern United States.

EXAMPLE: The Acid Rain Fiction

In order to develop information upon which intelligent policy could be made, the United States Congress funded a study spanning 10 years, costing 570 million dollars and employing more than three thousand scientists. This was the most careful and comprehensive acid rain study performed. The National Acid Precipitation Assessment Program (NAPAP) conducted the study and presented their results in 1990.[10] The goal was to get to the bottom of the so-called acid rain phenomenon. The study found that the danger of man-made acid rain was vastly overblown.

The comprehensive study did not impress Liberal activists. Many refused to accept the NAPAP results as valid, claiming that it did not gather enough data, that it was superficial and unreliable. Environmental activists tenaciously clung to the *political fiction* that the forests of the northeast were being destroyed by man-made acid rain. The acid rain fiction found its way into a friendly Liberal press.

Many journalists reported that smokestack industry was polluting the air and producing a man-made acid rain which was decimating the forests of the northeastern United States. These journalists had a high regard for studies and scientists who make such claims. But journalists discarded the massive evidence in the 10-year NAPAP study, choosing instead to rely on their political prejudices. They continued to perceive acid rain in the northeast United States long after the NAPAP study was released.

Remaining in denial, most of the mainstream press continued to report that man-made acid rain was falling on the forests of the northeast. Even though the results of the NAPAP study were presented on the CBS news program *60 Minutes* in December, 1990, and again in August, 1991, news coverage continued as if the *60 Minutes* piece had never aired. In her 1972 book on news making, author Edith Efron refers to this technique as "report and ignore". The press continues to present the acid rain fiction as if proven fact.

But sometimes unwanted facts can't be denied, ignored or forgotten. In that case the unwanted facts can be reinterpreted, reshaped or transformed. Likely we all learn this at an early age. Several years ago I heard a probably apocryphal story about a young child watching a movie. The image of a menacing snake suddenly appears on the screen. The young person at first reacts with fear but then says, "That snake loves me." If people are presented with information which they find uncomfortable, they may change its shape to make it more friendly.

EXAMPLE: The Bouncing Checks

In March of 1992 a scandal broke over the United States House of Representatives. Many congresspeople had been writing rubber checks on a little bank run by the House of Representatives. Disconcerting to the Liberal press, most of the leading check bouncers were Democrats. The so-called House bank did not make loans or pay interest. It really wasn't a bank, but it did provide a financial convenience for members of the House of Representatives. This House non-bank was managed by the Democrats since they were the ruling majority. So, the responsibility for this scandal was clearly in the lap of the Democrats.

This created a cognitive problem for the Liberal press. Remember that the partisan attitude of political Liberals dictates that Republicans are mostly dirty politicians and Democrats mostly are not. Thus, the image of sleazy House Democrats bouncing checks and getting away with it must not have been welcome news to the Liberal press. Clearly, this unwanted image needed to be reinterpreted.

Instead of pointing an accusatory finger at the Democrats, journalists claimed that "both sides were guilty." While this is sometimes an accurate assessment, it is often used by the guilty party to excuse his own wrongdoing. And that's exactly what House Democrats did with the enthusiastic help of the Liberal press. The press reinterpreted a situation in which one party (the Democrats) has the lion's share of guilt and made it appear as though Republicans were equally to blame.

Instead of painting a picture of scandalous behavior on the part of leading Democrats in the House of Representatives, journalists painted a picture of Democrats and Republicans engaged in the usual partisan warfare. Suppose this scandal had broken after the Republicans assumed leadership of the House in 1994, and *they* were the big check bouncers. I have no doubt that television journalists with wrinkled brows would have told us in a reproving voice all about ... *The Republican Check Kiting Scandal!*

We also enlist our memories in this self-serving effort to transform unwanted information into something more useful. Regardless of one's party affiliation or ideological inclination, real events sometimes work against us. But as time goes by we can recall those unwanted events differently than how they actually happened. We employ selective recall. What we happen to remember and how we remember it has a lot to do with what we want to believe. As discussed above, one of the things that partisan Democrats and journalists want to believe is that times were just awful during the 1980s.

EXAMPLE: Remembering the 1980s

When Republican Ronald Reagan assumed the presidency in 1981, Democrats and the press wanted to experience an economic dark age. But the economy did not cooperate. Reagan ended his presidency having presided over the longest peacetime economic expansion in history, creating some 18 million new jobs.[11] This was not welcome news for Democrats and their ideological soul mates in the press. How did the Liberal press turn good economic news into bad news? Easy. Partisan journalists simply transformed their memories of the 1980s.

If people made a lot of money, journalists interpreted that as a sign of greed. If people advanced in their careers, journalists interpreted that as a sign of selfishness. If jobs were created, the jobs were not worth having. By the 1990s, the Liberal press had developed this partisan reflex into a full-blown memory of *An Age of Greed*. Now, journalists routinely use expressions like, "the excesses of the 1980s." The decade has been derisively referred to as the "go-go 80s." There are many examples of back spin on the 1980s.

Consider this from Bryant Gumbel when he was on the NBC *Today Show*: "The greedy excesses of the Reagan years, the mean income of the average physician nearly doubled, from $88,000 to $170,000. Was that warranted?"[12] (Notice that journalists don't actually deny that the 1980s were good economic times.)

Or this comment that journalist Sam Donaldson made to Senator Robert Dole on the Sunday news show, *This Week With David Brinkley*, on February 21, 1993. "Senator, don't you believe, a lot of people do think that the '80s were an excess, which a lot of people got richer and people got poorer, and it's now fair to redress that balance?" [he probably meant to say "imbalance."]

Or this comment from journalist Bryant Gumbel on the *Today Show*, on January 22, 1993, "The boom years following World War Two saw the U. S. economy take off, giving the rise to the growth of the great American middle class. The rising standard of living meant homes, cars, TVs, college for the kids -- all in all, a piece of the American dream. But in the Reagan years, economic erosion set in, so much so that the middle class now finds itself in ever-deepening trouble."

Or this one from journalist Keith Morrison of NBC's "Nightly News," on February 7, 1993, "The amazing thing is most people seem content to believe that almost everybody had a good time in the '80s, a real shot at the dream. But the fact is, they didn't. Did we wear blinders? Did we think that the '80s just left behind the homeless? The fact is that almost nine in ten Americans actually saw their lifestyle decline." This partisan view of the 1980s tracks very closely to the party line of leading Democrats who selectively remember the 1980s in a way that feeds their political prejudices.

It is easy to spot the self-serving memories in other people. But we all alter memories to fit our political beliefs and partisan passions. Memory is very pliable. For instance, studies show that we actually change our memories to fit new information. Apparently, memory is a constructed interpretation of our past experiences, not a copy of it. Even though memory is annotated with all manner of biased interpretations, we tend to think our memories are accurate representations of past events. To illustrate the changing nature of our memories try the following demonstration.

Watch a newscast, say CNN's "Prime News" or *The CBS Evening News*. Pick a story about a controversy on which you have strong feelings, say abortion or gun control. Record the news story on your video cassette recorder (VCR). Wait an hour or so, and then write down what you remember about the news story and seal it in an envelope. Wait a week and again write down your memory of the newscast, sealing it also in an envelope. Wait a month and do the same thing. Now replay your video tape of the story and compare it to what you have written down. Did you remember the story in such a way as to fit nicely into your position on the issue? There is an excellent chance that you will see your memory develop and change, especially if you feel strongly about the subject matter in the story or the way the news story was presented.

This little demonstration leads to what I think is a fundamental error in how all of us, including journalists, think about our perceptions. We mistakenly think our perceptions are exact copies of reality when they are not. We discount the effect of biased thinking on what we perceive, while biases profoundly distort what we think we "see." All of us tend to have more confidence in our perceptions than is actually justified. I call this a fundamental perception error.

A FUNDAMENTAL PERCEPTION ERROR

As previously noted, journalists claim to leave their biases at the door when they come to work. Journalists claim that their Liberal opinions and support of Democratic Presidents do not prevent them from producing fair and balanced news. Journalists claim that, "... it is quite easy to put aside whatever political views or ideology we favor, ..."[13] However, the field of psychology provides good reason to believe that journalists fail miserably in that effort. Studies show that people, including journalists, are largely unaware of the subjective nature of their own perceptions. Thus, I think it fair to conclude that journalists underestimate the effect of their opinions on their perception of reality.[14]

In fact, journalists routinely take their opinions to be reality itself. They naively define bias as deviation from that reality. Conservative and Republican ideas are perceived to deviate from the truth. Eliminating bias in the news, means eliminating the Conservative and Republican influence in news making. This may only be a little tongue-in-cheek, but it does exhibit the serious problem journalists encounter when actually trying to drive bias out of their own thinking. It is very difficult for anyone to even become aware of their own biases.

Setting aside biases is difficult because perceiving is a circular process. Believing is seeing. Seeing reinforces beliefs. That is, journalists go to current events with their Liberal biases in hand. They perceive current events through those biases. Events are categorized accordingly, thus restricting the thematic framework of news stories. A Liberal version of events is the logical result. Journalists take their Liberal version of current events to be accurate representations of reality, thus validating the original Liberal beliefs. This circular process is exactly what makes journalists insensitive to their own biases.

In other words, for a journalist to become aware of his political biases, he must question his own axiomatic beliefs upon which his sense of reality is constructed. That's a tall order for anyone, let alone the arrogant opinionated Washington press corps. Taking their perception of political events to be objective reality, elite journalists are just not motivated to question their basic beliefs. On the contrary, they are motivated to present their beliefs to benighted news consumers as proven fact.

SUMMARY

Journalists claim that their political opinions do not affect the content of the news. Journalists claim to merely report what they observe or perceive. And that is the problem. There is plenty of evidence from the field of psychology to believe that the perceptions people have are quite faulty, providing reason to believe that **the Liberal opinions and partisan passions of leading journalists profoundly distort the production of news**. In fact, journalists make well-known mental errors as they observe newsworthy events and tell us about them.

An important group of errors is associated with labeling people and events. Like the rest of us, journalists attach labels which fit their beliefs and prejudices. The labels once attached to a news story, influence all subsequent information processing of that story. Inference biases and prejudiced judgements are also associated with the way people categorize (label) people and events.

Another group of errors is that of going beyond the facts they have in hand and coming up an unjustified explanation of current events. When seeking to confirm their prejudiced explanations, journalists likely come up with strategies designed to confirm their version of events.

Selection Bias

1. <u>Attach value to supporting information.</u> Information which supports a belief is deemed important and true.

2. <u>Devalue information which threatens a belief.</u> Threatening information can be avoided by using various dodges. So, unwanted information can be:

    a. Deemed incorrect or simply denied.
    b. Considered true but unimportant.
    c. Reinterpreted to bring it into conformance with opinion.
    d. Ignored or forgotten.
    e. Remembered differently.
    f. Conveniently misunderstood.

Journalists display an amazing capacity to select information which is consistent with partisan prejudices while, at the same time, finding ingenious ways to dismiss information which does not fit. It is important to note that people also employ selection bias in an effort to avoid connecting the dots, even when there is overwhelming evidence to do so.

Journalists maintain their political prejudices by tuning their eyes to perceive the things they want to see. They select information which makes vivid their Liberal beliefs. *Thus, journalists perceive a Liberal reality and produce a news that illuminates that reality*. Only after the information die is cast do journalists begin to think about fairness and balance. But that is too late. In the end, the uninhibited political prejudices of leading journalists transform real events into fictional versions of those events suitable for use by Democratic partisans and Liberal activists.

You don't need academic studies to see the Liberal bias in the news. Just listen to the way journalists explain events. Journalists explain that poverty causes crime. Journalists explain that a do-gooding Democratic President is opposed by a mean-spirited Republican Speaker of the House of Representatives out for himself.

When journalists hear of someone defending themselves with a firearm, they label him a vigilante. And they explain the abortion issue as a debate between good "pro-choice" activists opposed by bad "anti-abortionists." Only a Liberal journalist could perceive *Conservative* Communists after the fall of the Bolshevik cabal in the former Soviet Union.

On issue after issue the evening news will find some way to tell you that the Liberal point of view is correct and the Conservative point of view is wrong. Intentionally or not, the elite press constructs a news which stays within the contours of Liberal beliefs and the political prejudices of the left wing of the Democratic party. Knowledge of the political opinions and partisan sympathies of leading journalists can be used to predict how journalists will gather, construct and present the news.

DISCUSSION

The perception bias in the Liberal media is perfectly clear to any non-Liberal. When I started the task of writing this book, I did not seek to prove it but to explain it. First I turned to academic research in the field of journalism, thinking that some academic had already studied the subject. I found next to nothing. The very idea of Liberal bias was ridiculed by academics. One academic paper claimed that it was the news consumers who were biased. I then turned to the field of sociology. Again the information pickings were meager.

On the way back from the California Polytechnic University library at San Luis Obispo, California, I stopped at a used book store and happened upon *The News Twisters* by Edith Efron. By analyzing news content she made a case that the news had a definite Liberal tilt. Published in 1972, it was a ground-breaking book on media criticism. About that time *The Media Elite* by L. Robert Lichter, Linda Lichter and Stuart Rothman was published. They suggested that journalists were just as susceptible to selective perception as the rest of us. After some research into the subject of selective perception, I wrote a chapter entitled "Selection Bias."

However, as time passed, I decided that selection alone provided an inadequate explanation of what happens inside the heads of leading journalists. Lichter and colleagues had pointed me off in a new direction. I began searching the academic literature in the field of psychology. It was my intent to find research supporting the idea that the beliefs of journalists distort how they do their work. As I began that task, I found the monograph, *How Do Journalists Think*, by S. Holly Stocking and Paget H. Gross. It turned out that they had already done the job. Since most academics are politically Liberal, they may or may not approve of what I have done with their research.

In any case, it seems clear now that study in the field of psychology provides good reason to believe that the opinions of journalists distort the gathering of raw information and the production of news products. There is reason to believe that the unproven political opinions of leading journalists have a profound affect on the shape and content of the news.

In this chapter I have focused on the circular relationship between belief and perception. I have only touched on other mental tasks performed by journalists. An important task is to explain people and events. Those explanations are tested. Raw news information is selected and integrated into news products suitable for sale to the public. There are well-known biases and errors associated with the performance of all these tasks. (See

How Do Journalists Think by S. Holly Stocking and Paget H. Gross for a summary discussion of that work.)

Although most of this chapter rests on my interpretation of the psychological research and seems well founded, some elements are more speculative. One speculative idea is what I have called a *fundamental perception error*. In my opinion this error is just a formal statement of the implications of the research. Since I make no claims to be an academic who is aware of all the research in this field, I may be repeating someone else's work. The claims I make here are fairly narrow. I simply think it is sound to argue that people (including journalists) have a very difficult time looking past their fundamental beliefs, opinion, biases and prejudices.

END NOTES

(1) See page 111 of **How do Journalists Think**? A proposal for the Study of Cognitive Bias in Newsmaking. by S. Holly Stocking and Paget H. Gross; published by ERIC Clearinghouse on Reading and Communication Skills, Indiana University, Bloomington, Indiana in 1989.

(2) For a good survey of these mental tasks see, **How Do Journalists Think?**

(3) See pages 13 to 19 of **How do Journalists Think?** for a discussion of the cognitive task of categorizing. Categorizing involves what psychologists call "cognitive matching." A description of cognitive matching can be found in the appendix on page 111.

(4) See page 46 of **How do Journalists Think?**

(5) See the Joint Report of the Task Force to Investigate Certain Allegations Concerning the Holding of American Hostages by Iran in 1980, authored by the United States House of Representatives, Committee on Foreign Affairs, Lee H. Hamilton, chairman and Henry Hyde, ranking Republican. Dated January 3, 1993. House Report number 102-1102. Library of Congress Call Number: E183.8 I55 U53 1993. This document can acquired from the Government Printing Office or your nearest university library.

(6) See the network broadcasts for May 28, 1996 and *U. S. News & World Report* for June 10, 1996, page 32.

(7) See page 16 of **How do Journalists Think?** For further reading see the academic paper by Bransford, J. D. & Franks, J. J. titled <u>The Abstraction of Linguistic ideas</u> in the journal *Cognitive Psychology* dated 1971. Also see the academic paper by Cantor, N. & Mischel, W. titled <u>Trials as Prototypes: Effects on Recognition Memory</u> in the *Journal of Personality and Social Psychology* dated 1977.

(8) For a good discussion of the preference for Liberal sources see pages 55 to 63 of **The Media Elite** by S. Robert Lichter, Stanley Rothman and Linda S. Lichter; published by Adler and Adler, Bethesda, Maryland in 1986.

(9) The "ability to avoid perceiving dissonant information while at the same time absorbing ideas that we agree with is known as selective perception." The idea is that contrary information creates a cognitive dissonance. The contrary information runs counter to some belief. That is, both the belief and the contrary information can't <u>both</u> be true, thus creating the "cognitive dissonance."

For a discussion of selective perception see, **Mass Media Systems and Effects**, written by Phillips W. Davison; James Boylan and Frederick T. C. Yu; published by Praeger Publishers of New York, in 1976, starting at page 135.

(10) The <u>Final Assessment Reports</u> of the National Acid Precipitation Assessment Program (NAPAP) can be purchased from the Superintendent of Documents, Government Printing Office, Washington, DC 20402-9325. One might also contact NAPAP, Office of the Director, 722 Jackson Place, NW, Washington, DC 20503 for acid rain information.

(11) See **What Went Right in the 1980s**, by Professor Richard B. McKenzie, Published by the Pacific Research Institute for Public Policy, San Francisco, California, 1994.

(12) See NBC's "Today Show" for March 31, 1993.

(13) This is a quote from Don Baker, Richmond, Virginia, Bureau Chief of the Washington Post which aired on C-SPAN on July 11, 1996 as part of its "Washington Journal."

(14) It was "the fundamental attribution error" from psychology which inspired me to call this mental error, the fundamental perception error. The fundamental attribution error is the tendency of people to underestimate the effect of situational forces on individual behavior. See a basic text in social psychology.

Chapter 3

PARTISAN BIAS

Journalists claim to be non-partisan because they do not openly endorse candidates for public office or use obviously partisan language. But this is an overly narrow idea of what it means to be partisan. One need not openly endorse a political candidate to *suggest* that people ought to vote for that candidate. Partisan speech need not employ obvious ideological language. Partisan speech may even sound quite neutral. However, close examination of the speech patterns of politicians and political activists reveals what we all recognize as partisan, that is, an "us versus them" attitude.

This "us versus them" attitude is based on a bigoted mythology common to most political factions, Conservative Republicans, Liberal Democrats, various political interest groups, etc. The mythology assumes a familiar form. Partisans reflexively blame enemy out-groups for everything bad while taking credit for everything good. Partisans see themselves in an epic battle against the forces of darkness with the fate of good society in the balance. Partisans go to this battle with an unquestioned mandate to govern the people.[1]

The partisan mandate can be summarized as follows: *1) in-group heros cause all the good things to happen, 2) out-group partisans cause all the bad things to happen so, 3) let the in-group run the country (without serious opposition) and they will build the good society.* Only the in-group can make the world a better place.

Thus, political out-groups never have legitimate claim to power and can only win public office by deceit and dirty tricks. The idea is that ordinary people would never vote for an opposition bad guy if they really knew what he was all about. Partisans often claim that an enemy win on election day is not an affirmation of his ideas or policies, because they had misled the voters in what amounts to election fraud. A version of this partisan attitude surfaced in the press when Conservative Republican Ronald Reagan was elected President.

Reagan won overwhelming electoral victories when he ran for President in 1980 and 1984. However, the Liberal press declared that Reagan had no true mandate from the people. The reasoning was that people voted for President Reagan because they liked him, not because they agreed with his wrongheaded Conservative policies. From this partisan view, President Reagan never legitimately exercised power, because his policies were never truly ratified by the people. Thus Republicans had no mandate to implement their ideas.

When Liberal Democrat William Jefferson Clinton was elected President in 1992, the press did a flip-flop. The same elite journalists now found a mandate in the 43 percent vote President Clinton received. They eagerly gave Democrat Clinton the mandate they denied to Republican Reagan. In the months shortly after the 1992 election, many journalists said something like this, "Clinton campaigned on his policies. Since Clinton was elected President, the country should go along with his policies." The elite press has often expressed the Clinton mandate in this backhanded manner.

It was a happy time for the press and the Democrats. The glowing year-end reviews for 1992 and 1993 reflect this newfound optimism. It is part of the mythology. When the forces of goodness and light are in power, it is a golden age. The golden age that stands out for political Liberals, including those in the press, is the reign of President John F. Kennedy (1961-1963). That time has since become known as "Camelot." You will remember that Camelot is the site of the palace of the mythical King Arthur. The word "Camelot" has come to mean a time of idyllic happiness, a golden age. The Arthurian legend reveres great heroes who do great deeds. Likewise, political partisans honor the accomplishments of their heroes. Some of this partisan hero worship is passed off as news.

EXAMPLE: Hero Robert Kennedy

Since the 1960s the Kennedys have been favorite heroes of the Liberal press. So it is not surprising that on the twenty-fifth anniversary of the assassination of Democrat Robert Kennedy, the press treated us to a number of loving "news reports" detailing his great accomplishments. There was no pretense of journalism. NBC News was in fact celebrating and honoring the life of Liberal Democrat Robert Kennedy.

On May 28, 1993, NBC's "Today Show" aired a program called "The Legacy of Robert Kennedy." The softball interview with three of Robert Kennedy's grown children was conducted by Katie Couric. A large portrait of Robert Kennedy on the wall set a reverent tone. Ms. Couric identified Kennedy as a good guy by her line of questions and comments. She referred to his desire to "help the needy, the underprivileged." The theme of the interview was how these Democrats, Robert Kennedy and his children, have worked to make the world a better place.[2]

The reverent tone did not prevent a little Republican bashing, however. Speaking in linguistic code, Kerry Kennedy Cuomo, daughter of Robert Kennedy, referred to, "the divisiveness which we have seen, especially over the last 12 years, the dark side of America, what you see in people like ... David Duke, but also in more mainstream politicians."

Let me translate. Referring to the "last 12 years" is code for "the Reagan/Bush years." Ms. Cuomo is apparently trying to say that Republicans Reagan and Bush represent "the dark side of America" and are responsible for "the divisiveness," in the country. The reference to known racist David Duke suggests that Republicans Reagan and Bush fostered racism and are probably racists themselves. By allowing this partisan comment to stand without rebuttal, journalist Couric implied that Reagan and Bush were political villains. Journalists do not let such comments about leading Democrats go unchallenged.

Democrats and elite journalists typically perceive Republicans as villains. For example, when Republican Newt Gingrich became Speaker of the United States House of Representatives, the press constructed villainous images of him. *Time* Magazine ran a cover with a cartoon caricature of Gingrich as a Mr. Scrooge who has just broken Tiny Tim's crutch in a fit of Republican mean-spiritedness. *Newsweek* also ran a political cartoon on its cover. They turned Speaker Gingrich into the evil Grinch from the Dr. Seuss Christmas story. Making a play on the two names, the *Newsweek* cover read, "The Gingrich That Stole Christmas."

Partisans recognize only the accomplishments of their own heroes. Thus, out-group Republicans are seen by Liberal journalists as making little positive contribution to society. Little good happens when they run things.

Republicans destroy the fabric of society. That is, Republicans are dangerous, even when well intentioned. That's why Democrats perceived a dark age descending on the country when Republican Ronald Reagan became President. This partisan myth became proven fact by the time it found its way to the evening news.

EXAMPLE: The Decade of Greed

Democrats labeled the eight years of Conservative Republican Ronald Reagan (1981-1989), as a "Decade of Greed." In a stump speech given on March 6, 1992, candidate William Clinton said that making the quick buck was a dominant value promoted by leading Republicans during the 1980s. He argued that children see on television that selling drugs is a way to make a fast buck, thus leading his audience to believe that Republicans were responsible for drug crime during the 1980s.

The elite press continues to propagate this same partisan mythology. They tell us that the 1980s was a time of "excesses and shortsightedness," "a-something-for-nothing-decade" when "junk bond values were incorporated into policy." During this "greed is good decade," we had "a smoke and mirrors prosperity which left the country holding the bag," with "the inner cities ... in a grip of selfishness brought about by the Republicans." It was "a time when greed and self-interest ran amok."[3]

The political myth that times are good when Democrats run things and bad when Republicans run things is apparently quite real to many journalists. When moving from a *Republican dark age* to *Democratic good times*, one would expect journalists to perceive a sudden change for the better. Indeed, that was the case after election day 1992. Remember that Republican George Bush lost the election to Democrat William Clinton. Up to election day in November, 1992, the press was reporting an economy in serious trouble. Virtually the day after the election, the Liberal press began detecting a new optimism in the country. Hope. The press reported that the economy was getting better even before Democrat Clinton was sworn in as President. It seemed that the country had turned the corner. Happy days were here again.

REPUBLICANS DON'T ACCOMPLISH MUCH

One of the reasons times are bad when Republicans run things is that they don't accomplish much. Or at least that's the way some journalists seem to see it. Even when Republicans actually do accomplish something, the press will find a way to say they really didn't. A good example of this rhetorical trickery was the press coverage of the Republican Contract For America.

When the Republicans took over the United States House of Representatives in 1994, they introduced ten items for an up or down vote. The items were: (1) balanced budget amendment and line item veto, (2) anti-crime measures, (3) welfare reform, (4) protecting kids, (5) tax cuts for families, (6) increase national security funding, (7) raise senior citizens' earning limit, (8) roll back government regulations, (9) stop excessive legal claims and (10) congressional term limits.[4]

The context for making this promise is that for years the Democratically-controlled House of Representatives had kept these items bottled up in committee and would not allow a floor vote. Republicans knew from polling data that these items were very popular with the public. The Republicans promised to at least bring them up for a floor vote and did so in the first one hundred days of the new 104th Congress. House Republicans did it. They fulfilled the contract. The Liberal press had a problem. How to say that Congressional Republicans had done nothing.

Of course they found a way. Like the Democrats, journalists began saying that *The Contract was a failure because all of it did not become law.* (That, of course, was not in the contract.) For a bill to become law it must pass both the House of Representatives and the Senate and then be signed by the President. The President in 1994 was a Democrat, William Jefferson Clinton. Journalists claimed that the people were expecting the Contract with America to become law. Not all of it become law. Therefore, House Republicans did not perform. This sophistry is how journalists were able to claim that Republicans did not fill their Contract.

DEMOCRATS HAVE ALTRUISTIC MOTIVES

Democrats constantly question the motives of Republicans, while claiming to be selfless servants of the people. Democratic partisans attribute the best motives to themselves and the worst motives to their Republican opposition. Democrats perceive themselves as pure-hearted people acting only out of principle. But the motives of Republicans are always suspect. Democrats perceive Republicans as selfish people who seek political power for personal gain. This partisan stereotype is also seen in the Liberal press.

Listening to the news, one would think that Democrats always act out of altruistic motives. Starting with the 1992 election campaign, the Liberal press has unceasingly characterized the motives of Democrat Clinton as good. According to many journalists, Democrat Clinton is dedicated to doing good. For instance, journalist Lisa Myers of NBC had this to say during the 1992 campaign, "Throughout his life he has been committed to public service and doing good."[5] This little testimonial was not an isolated comment in the press coverage. Clinton was rarely accused of having the sinister motives with which the Liberal press regularly attributed to Republican candidate George Bush.

Contrast, for instance, how the press explains political disputes between the President and his opposition in the United States Congress. When Republican Presidents Ronald Reagan and George Bush were opposed by Congressional Democrats, the press characterized their political activity as *principled opposition.* That is, Congressional Democrats were acting out of good motives. How did the press characterize Congressional Republicans when Liberal Democrat William Clinton was elected in 1992? The press characterized Congressional Republicans as *obstructionist.* In other words, Republicans were not acting out of good motives.

It is characteristically partisan to attribute bad motives to political out-groups. The notion that one political party acts from good motives and the other does not comes from a prejudiced habit of thought. The truth is that various politicians act out of all kinds of motives. Some have good motives, some don't. Some of those with bad motives are Republicans and some are Democrats. Some with bad motives are Liberals and some are Conservatives. Thus, *journalists exhibit a partisan bias by constantly attributing unsavory, unprincipled or selfish motives to leading Republicans while attributing good motives to Democrats.*

DEMOCRATS USUALLY TELL THE TRUTH

A liar is someone who consistently tells untruths with the knowledge that what he is saying is false. Thus a person can tell an untruth without being a liar, if he has no knowledge of that untruth and has no intent to deceive. When someone makes an untrue statement with the knowledge of its untruth, then he is telling a lie. But he is not a liar unless he makes a habit of it.

I would extend that idea to include people who tell less than *the whole truth* with intent to deceive others. One of the most common "truth telling lies" is to tell only part of the truth. That is why people are sworn to "tell the truth and the whole truth" before testifying in a court of law. Telling a half-truth is a pernicious form of lying. In other words, deception is a lie. People who deliberately and consciously deceive others are liars, regardless of how they accomplish their deception.

The truth about telling the truth is that some people tell the truth, some shade the truth, some dance around it, some make statements with purpose of evasion, some lie a little and others lie a lot. Some of these people are Republicans, some are Democrats, some are Conservatives while others are Liberals. No group of any size has a monopoly on either truth telling or lying. If politicians were not allowed to tell a half-truth with intent to deceive, they would most likely have little to say during their short political campaign. That's just the nature of politics in a large country with diverse constituencies.

Many, if not most, politicians and activists lie according to this definition. They do it unhesitatingly in what they consider a good cause. I don't think they even consider it lying. If caught in this activity, partisans will find some way to explain it away. They might turn the lie into a virtue and say that it was the right thing to do. Or they may "cop to a lesser plea" and admit to some small inconsistencies, while claiming to be fundamentally truthful. Or they may try to assign blame to some vague unknown person by saying that "mistakes were made." Or they may use the "everybody does it" excuse. When Democrats employ these rhetorical tactics, the press will tell us that it does not matter.

EXAMPLE: <u>Covering Untruths Told by Democrats</u>

The essence of media bias is that the press strongly tends to cover Republicans differently than Democrats. Since he began his campaign for the presidency in 1992, journalists have treated untruths told by President Clinton as unimportant, a bad habit like eating junk food, not representative of anything serious.

When responding to a viewer call on the old CNN's "Sonya Live," journalist Friedman excuses Clinton's shading of the truth by saying, "When you tell people that you are going to do a variety of things, and they don't see you do it, even if it is more complicated than you knew getting in, maybe you were too green."

Bob Cohen of *Newsweek* responded with this comment about Clinton's creative relationship with the truth, "It's the most obvious news story to do, to compare campaign pledges to reality. And it's been done and we'll continue to do it. Now *we've* [my emphasis] only been in for five months. And I think that one thing reporters have not been fair about is giving him a chance to get some of his package in place. But, when Doctor Learner [another guest on the show] talks about everything that Reagan and Bush did in terms of deception, what we are criticizing President Clinton for the most part is the sense of incompetence at the White House, the sense of being all thumbs, the Kimba Wood and the Zoe Baird, Air Force One, a hair cut, the Travelgate situation. *We are not talking about deception.* [my italics] This is not Iran/Contra. This is a sense that they haven't quite got their act together."

Ms. Friedman is claiming that President Clinton merely underestimated the difficulties of getting things done as President and that he had no intent to deceive the public about what he was going to do as President. Mr. Cohen supports this view by saying that the Clinton crew was all thumbs, not real liars like the Reagan and Bush people.

In contrast to the ho-hum attitude that journalists display towards untruths promoted by Democrats is the hostile attitude of the elite press toward untruths promoted by Republicans. As with most partisan Democrats, *Republican lies are deemed important by the press, because those lies are perceived as symptomatic of deeper wrong-doing.* (Of course, Conservative journalists would see Democratic lies as symptomatic of deeper wrong-doing.) During the campaign season, Democrats and Liberal journalists may seize on the smallest inconsistency in the language of a leading Republican as proof of an intent to deceive the public in a corrupt pursuit of power.

EXAMPLE: Reporting on Untruths told by Republicans

During the 1992 presidential campaign the *MacNeil/Lehrer News Hour* aired a panel discussion of the then-Democratic candidate for President, Governor William Clinton of Arkansas. One of the panelists, Mr. Paul Greenberg of the *Arkansas Democrat-Gazette*, was very critical of Clinton and said he had "never been able to find a single coherent principle at the core of [Clinton's] politics that [Greenberg] could feel confident that [Clinton] would not sacrifice in the heat of battle for another political office." *News/Hour* journalist Judy Woodruff, now with CNN, responded with emotion in her voice saying, "That's a ... really ... stiff charge to make against somebody. What do you base that on? 'Never a principle he is willing to stick with?'"[6]

Not more than a few minutes later, another member of the panel, Roy Wilkins of George Mason University said, "George Bush has demonstrated in the last four years that he has neither the character nor the judgement to be President of the United States. He demonstrated by picking Dan Quayle. He demonstrated by lying to us in one sentence by saying that Clarence Thomas is the best qualified man in the country to be on the Court and that race wasn't a factor, and he demonstrated by going to Rio and disgracing us." Ms. Woodruff had nothing to say about this latter partisan invective.

What has Woodruff communicated by this verbal behavior? She expressed emotional and verbal disbelief when a panelist said that Democrat William Clinton was a cynical politician lacking in character. But when somebody said that Republican George Bush was a lying deceitful person, Woodruff allowed that accusation to stand. Taken together, this verbal behavior generates the message that Republican Bush lacks the character (including truth telling) to be President while Democrat Clinton is fully qualified.

The tendentious coverage of political lying is typical of the partisan style of thinking. We are told that Democrats only tell fibs about unimportant subjects. The press leads us to believe that these little deviations from the truth are not connected to any serious character flaws that might influence job performance of said Democrats. However, the press tells us that lies coming out of the Republican camp are of a wholly different nature. Those lies are very important because they result from underlying character flaws that can have disastrous consequences on the job performance of Republican office holders. Partisan Democrats may also take Republican lies as evidence of dirty politics.

REPUBLICANS PLAY DIRTY

The idea that one political party plays dirty and the other one does not taps into the essence of political prejudice. Journalists seem totally unaware of their prejudices. They take it as a given that Republicans tend to be dirty players in the political process and Democrats tend to be clean players. The Liberal press explains dirty politics as if the Democrats were always the victim of Republican dirty tricks.

For instance, many journalists allege that Republicans use "wedge issues" to divide and conquer the electorate along racial lines in a callous pursuit of political power. For many journalists, a television ad used during the 1988 presidential campaign has become the noun for this invidious technique of Republican dirty play.

EXAMPLE: <u>The Willy Horton Ad</u>

Many Democrats and Liberal-minded journalists believe that Governor Michael Dukakis lost the presidential election in 1988, because he did not answer the Republican attacks quickly enough, thus allowing the Republicans to define him as a "soft on crime" Liberal Democrat. According to this partisan view of the election, Republicans fanned racist fears of black criminals in a cynical appeal to the dark side of the electorate.

In the 1980s, Mr. Willy Horton was a convicted murderer residing in the prison system of Massachusetts. He was let out of prison on a furlough while Michael Dukakis was governor. While on a furlough from prison term, Horton severely victimized a family. The Willy Horton story provided good media fodder for those who wanted to attack Liberal politicians on the crime issue. But *it was Democrat Albert Gore who first raised the furlough issue in 1988!* However, you would be hard pressed to learn that fact from the evening news.

In fact, the furlough program had been an issue in Massachusetts the previous year. In 1987 a Massachusetts newspaper, the *Eagle-Tribune*, published some 175 articles about Horton, his victims and the furlough program. The story was hard to get. Governor Dukakis did not cooperate. He refused to meet with crime victims. But *Eagle-Tribune* journalists did get the furlough story and in 1987 won a Pulitzer Prize for it.

While running in a 1988 presidential primary against Governor Dukakis, the opposition research team of Senator Albert Gore of Tennessee discovered the Horton furlough issue. Gore used it in his losing bid for the presidency. A Republican attack information team also came across this juicy piece of information.[7]

Later, Republicans used the attack information during the general election of 1988. Republicans produced a paid campaign advertisement which attacked the Democrat, Governor Dukakis, as "soft on crime." The ad run by the Republican campaign featured what appeared to be a prison with a turnstile. Criminals going in and coming right back out. A voice over carried a Republican campaign message. The apparent intention (in my opinion) was to dramatize the accusation that Democrats are soft on crime.

There were actually two Willy Horton ads. The one that most people saw was run nationally by the formal Republican campaign. It contained no picture of Willy Horton. The other ad was run only in California by a rump political group which supported the Republican ticket. It had a similar soft on crime message but featured a picture of the African-American Horton at the end of the ad.

Republicans and Democrats perceive the ad differently. It is instructive to take a look at these conflicting perceptions. Democrats are anxious to see the ad as racist. They claim it appeals to white fears of black criminals. They validate their claim merely by noting that Horton is an African-American. The ad is perceived by Democrats as just one more example of how Republicans use the politics of division and intolerance. This phrase, "the politics of division," is code for saying that Republicans and especially Conservative Republicans are racists. So the name "Willy Horton" has become a code for racially divisive Republican attack ads.[8]

The Republican perception is different, of course. They perceive the Horton ad to be about crime control. From this perception, letting Horton out of prison to commit more crime is a metaphor for what's wrong with Liberal thinking that seems to value the rights of criminals over the rights of law-abiding citizens. Every bit as partisan, Republicans perceived a callous indifference on the part of Liberal Democrats, which endangered the safety of ordinary citizens. Thus the Horton furlough was a legitimate campaign issue.

News accounts favored the partisan Democratic perception that the Willy Horton ad was an attempt to capitalize on racism. The press usually aired the rump ad instead of the official Republican campaign ad and implied that it was used by the official Republican campaign. The press led news consumers to believe that the official Republican campaign had produced the rump ad that featured the race of Willy Horton. Yet, Liberal journalists presented no evidence to support its sinister interpretation of the Republican ad.

Democrats perceive themselves in a perpetual state of fighting back with the truth after the Republicans started a campaign of smears and lies. Democrats don't perceive themselves as making mean-spirited attacks on Republicans. Even when the record clearly shows that a Democrat started the mud slinging, in-group Democrats still perceive the Republicans starting the dirty stuff. This is not an unknown response. It is called, *it started when he hit me back.* The sequence of events often goes like this. A Democrat will make a vicious verbal attack on an enemy Republican. However, Democrats perceive their words not as mudslinging but a statement of truth. The Republicans counterattack the Democrats. Now, the Democrats perceive this Republican attack as the beginning of the fight.

Let me illustrate the "it started when he hit me back" excuse. Democrats perceived the urban policies of presidents Reagan and Bush as the contributing factor in the 1992 Los Angeles Riot. Republican policies are viewed as insensitive to the true needs of the people of the inner city. The Republicans similarly view the Democrats as insensitive to the plight of the inner cities. The Republican view is that the Liberal welfare state dependence destroys the family structure and civilizing values. Riots in the inner city is the natural result.

The chronology of the partisan accusations and counter accusations that followed the Los Angeles Riots is revealing. On Sunday, May 3rd, just a of couple of days after the riots, candidate William Clinton suggested that the urban policies of Republican Presidents had created an environment in the minority communities of the inner cities which fostered severe hopelessness which finally resulted in a riot. This was the first shot fired. No doubt Democrats and elite journalists perceived the accusation as the truth, not a cheap shot. The Republican White House was outraged at the accusation. So on Monday, May 4th, White House press secretary Marlon Fitzwater told journalists that the failures of the Democratic Great Society welfare programs fostered the cycle of poverty.

Since Democrats perceived candidate Clinton's remark as the simple truth, they saw Fitzwater's remarks as the first punch. The press explained the riots in the same partisan fashion. The press also saw Fitzwater's criticism as the first punch. The evening news on Monday May 4th, Tuesday the 5th and Wednesday 6th, reflected this view. The evening news seemed to be saying that Republican Bush had thrown the first punch in a partisan round of fingerprinting and blaming.

The "it started when he hit me back" phenomenon is one more example of how journalists construct the news from the partisan perspective of a Liberal Democrat. Even though it is an obvious partisan perception, the press takes it as proven fact that Republicans play really dirty and the Democrats only play a little dirty. However, the truth is likely a little more dull. It is probably true that every political party has *only* its share of dirty players. It is just not believable, in my view, that nearly all the serious dirty players are either Republicans or Democrats.

REPUBLICANS RARELY DESERVE ANY RESPECT

Having accepted as fact that Republican are unprincipled liars who play dirty, it is easy to conclude that Republicans are beyond the pale of decent treatment. There is no imperative to be fair. If the rights of a

Republican are violated, it does not really matter. They got what's coming to them for the many things for which they did not get caught.

Republicans as bad guys, should not be allowed to even say the correct thing. Accordingly Republicans still don't have a right to speak, even when they are correct on the issues! Consider the treatment of Vice President Dan Quayle by the press in May and June of 1992. In the presidential campaign of that year, Quayle referred to "family values." He was roundly trashed by the elite press until journalists started talking to the voters about the subject. Consider the following highly editorialized copy from the June 8th, 1992 of *Newsweek* is illustrative, "... Dan Quayle-- flawed, callow, vehicle that he may be--seems to have nudged presidential politics perilously close to something that really matters, something perhaps too precious to be entrusted to mere politicians. The stolid, secure two-parent family Quayle posited as an antidote to urban violence and moral decay is a symbol that cuts very close to the bone."

However, *the Democrats always deserve respect.* That is why it is very important for everybody to be fair to Democrats. Good people always deserve to be treated fairly. Liberal Democrats do good work and it is important that they get a fair shake. The press treats allegations of wrongdoing Democrats with great suspicion. The evidence required to *prove* that a Democrat has engaged in wrongdoing is very substantial.

SUMMARY

Partisan speech is tricky. While innocent sounding, closer examination often reveals an "us versus them" attitude that characterizes partisan bias. It has several themes starting with the myth that the partisan in-group is the only true and just inheritor of political power. Enemy partisans are seen as usurping pretenders who can't win a fair election. If enemy partisans win, it is because they played dirty or appealed to the dark side of the electorate. Partisans of all stripes--Republicans, Democrats, Liberals and Conservatives--buy into this partisan mythology.

Elements of partisan bias are seen in news products. Often this "us versus them" attitude characterizes the press coverage of the political process, with Democrats as "us" and Republicans as "them." In fact, a deep-seated, pro-Democratic partisan bias infuses the entire press establishment.

Patterns of that bias are easily spotted. We are told that: (1) Democrats are the true representatives of the people, while Republicans represent narrow selfish interests. (2) Republicans tell big bad lies and Democrats tell little white lies, (3) Republicans play really dirty while Democrats only play a little dirty in self-defense and (4) the motives of Democrats are virtuous while Republican motives are selfish. In addition, many journalists use the word "conservative" as a synonym for "bad" and the word "liberal" as a synonym for "good."

Such political myths are common to the Liberal wing of the Democratic party. These partisan perspectives are a staple of political reporting. The imagery and messages of the evening news consistently convey the partisan myth that the Democrats are the good guys and the Republicans are the bad guys. That is, journalists explain events from the point of view of a Liberal Democrat.

Journalists pretend to be nonpartisan but their partisan attitude gives them away. A Liberal journalist will always find some way to tell news consumers that Republicans are the bad guys and Democrats are the good guys. This makes sense. Studies have shown that over the years elite journalists consistently vote for the Democrat for president by some 80 to 90 percent. A poll conducted by the Freedom Forum in March of 1996 showed that 89 percent of elite Washington-based correspondents had voted for Democrat William Clinton for president in 1992. The Freedom Forum is "a nonpartisan, international foundation." The work of the foundation is supported by an endowment established by Frank E. Gannett in 1935. It is not some kind of right wing political group, quite to the contrary.

DISCUSSION

The original inspiration for this chapter comes from Edith Efron's book *The News Twisters*. In that book she talks about two techniques of news bias, "glamorizing" and "deglamorizing." I observed that elite journalists tend to glamorize Liberal Democrats and deglamorize Conservative Republicans. Explaining this behavior as a result of ideological bias was not satisfying. It was not until I began to look at media bias as a form of political prejudice that I got a better explanation.

The idea behind ethnocentrism, the tendency to glorify one's own group while denigrating out-groups, seemed to provide a better explanation of "glamorizing" and "deglamorizing." As discussed in the previous chapter, I claim that there is a political version of ethnocentrism, cultural-centrism. What now seems more likely is that "glamorizing" and "deglamorizing" can be explained by the prejudiced tendency to glorify the political in-group while denigrating political out-groups.

I derived the individual characteristics of partisan bias from my own informal observations of strong partisans. I observed a common pattern of speech. Certain partisan themes seemed to repeat themselves. Strong partisans seemed to yearn for a simplistic explanation of human conflict. The interesting thing was that all partisans from all political parties on all sides of all the issues exhibited the same sort of predictable verbal behavior. I found that same partisan mind-set in the elite press. Amazingly, leading journalists repeat these same simplistic themes in their newscasts, providing good evidence that Liberal political prejudices are the source of media bias.

END NOTES

(1) Such mythology is central to the prejudiced style of thinking. Political combatants often yield to the easy vision of good versus evil. However, this is not to say the world is without evil. Truly good people are often compelled to struggle against people who are truly evil. The hot war against Adolf Hitler and the Cold War against Joseph Stalin are two good examples. The problem is that everyday partisans often turn conflicts between opposing political camps into a titanic struggle between good and evil. While colorful and sometimes great fun, the flamboyant partisan imagery often conceals a mean-spirited political bigotry.

(2) Later that night, NBC presented an hour-long "news" special "Robert F. Kennedy: The Man and His Memories," which shamelessly promoted Kennedy as a great American legend. Certifiably partisan political opinion was presented as proven fact.

(3) See the Media Research Center publication, <u>Notable Quotables</u>.

(4) See **Contract With America** by the Republican National Committee, published by Random House, in 1994.

(5) See the Lisa Myers report on NBC's "Nightly News" for October 21, 1992.

(6) See PBS's "MacNeil/Lehrer News Hour" of July 1992.

(7) See pages 49 through 55 of the Summer 1996 issue of the _Forbes Media Critic_, Volume 3, Number 4.

(8) Code word messages are usually directed to a particular group about another group. For instance, a Liberal politician may refer to a Republican as *Conservative* when talking to a minority group. In that case the word *Conservative* is code for racist. This is slick because Conservatives identify themselves as conservatives. Code words are hard to defend against.

Chapter 4

IDEOLOGICAL BIAS

For many years elite journalists denied that they were political Liberals. Denials continued, even after the ground breaking 1987 study by Professors Robert Lichter, Linda Lichter and Stanley Rothman demonstrated that, "The media elite are a group apart--urban and cosmopolitan in background, liberal and skeptical in outlook, self-involved and aggressive in personal style."[1] In their comprehensive book, *The Media Elite*, they reported that some 80 to 90 percent of leading journalists consistently voted for the Democrat for President over a period of many years.[2]

But by 1996 the phalanx of denials began to crack. CBS journalist Bernard Goldberg broke ranks and reported on the editorial page of the *Wall Street Journal* of February 13th. "The old argument that the networks and other 'media elites' have a liberal bias is so blatantly true that it's hardly worth discussing any more. No, we don't sit around in dark corners and plan strategies on how we're going to slant the news. We don't have to. It comes naturally to most reporters."

In March, 1996, the Freedom Foundation released a study which found that 89 percent of Washington journalists voted for Democrat William Clinton. This was not late breaking news. It supports the findings of the Lichter study a decade earlier. However, the Freedom Foundation has credibility with the press. A few journalists began to admit press Liberalism. Commenting on the article by Bernard Goldberg, the co-host for ABC's "Good Morning America" Charles Gibson said, "I don't deny for a minute that the basic bent of most journalists is liberal." He then went on to pooh-pooh any bad effect that fact might have on Republican presidential candidate Robert Dole.[3]

Admitting that they were political Liberals after all, the elite press secured the next logical fallback position. *Now journalists make the claim that their Liberal opinions do not leak into the news.* This is a remarkably false claim. In the second chapter I showed that there is good reason from the field of psychology to believe that Liberal opinion does in fact distort the evening news. And in the third chapter I suggested that an "us versus them" partisan prejudice often distorts the news. In this chapter I will show that Liberal ideology also distorts the news.

The word "ideology" comes from the word idea. My dictionary says that "ideology" refers to a "systematic body of concepts," "the thinking characteristic of an individual or group." Thus a political ideology is a systematic body of political concepts. The nuance of the meaning is that the ideas are integrated into a thoughtful whole. That's how the word is used here.[4]

Most partisan factions are identified by the collection of ideas they consider to be revealed truth. It is fundamental that competing partisans have different concepts of life, its problems, and what to do about them. The collection of ideas espoused by most Republicans is known as Conservative ideology. The collection of ideas promoted by most Democrats is known as Liberal ideology. Partisans consistently take sides on the hot issues of the day, and that is the key to ideological bias in the press.

If there were no ideological bias, news stories would not take sides on the issues. But journalists do take sides. Consider this amazing admission from ABC journalist Ann Compton, "In terms of how we cover the national scene, and the national presidential campaigns, I think it's true that we tend to take, ... we tend to go into issues stories with kind of a preconceived idea that one side of the issue is the logical right one ... the logical wrong one."[5] Compton claims that this issue bias is separate from any political bias. She denies that there is any political bias in the press. However, journalists consistently conceive that the Liberal Democrats are logically right and Conservative Republicans are logically wrong.

If there were no consistent political bias in the news, as Compton claims, different journalists would think that different sides of the issues are logically correct. But that is not the case. Take the issue of crime, for instance. If there were no consistent ideological bias, different news stories would attribute different causes to crime. One news story would assume that poverty causes crime, as Liberals believe. Another news story would assume that the disintegration of moral fiber causes crime, as Conservatives believe. Another news story might take an agnostic position and assume that the ultimate cause of crime is not known. Yet another news story might assume the only a little is known about the causes of crime. But the news about crime reflects no such distribution of ideas. News stories consistently attribute poverty as the cause of crime. In other words, the evening news tells us that the Liberal idea about crime (usually promoted by Democrats) is the correct one.

Do journalists side with Democrats on *all* the issues? In the 1992 presidential election they did. "On all major domestic issues in the campaign -- the economy, abortion, health care, education and the environment -- the news gave Clinton credit for better policies than the President [Republican George Bush]."[6]

However, you don't need an academic study to validate the ideological bias for yourself. Listen to the talk news, *CNN & Co*. ABC's "This Week," PBS's "Washington Week in Review," and observe what elite journalists consider to be undeniably true. Judge for yourself if journalists assume that Liberal ideas are proven fact. Observe news stories about the issues of crime, the economy, war, peace, size and role of government, and abortion and judge for yourself which side journalists consistently tell us is logically correct. Consider the ever-present issue of the size and scope of government.

THE WELFARE STATE IS GOOD

Liberals don't trust ordinary people to do the "right" thing. They seem to think that people can't protect themselves from poverty, bad health, criminals and sleazy businessmen. Liberals think that private action to solve social problems rarely turns out well. Liberals think it is their social responsibility to take care of ordinary people. The primary instrument for the job, in their opinion, is the federal government. *It is characteristic of the authoritarian style of thinking to want to use the power of government to force people to conform to some utopian vision of a good society.*

Liberals and other leftists have a fundamental perception in common. Liberals are among those who perceive social chaos in the absence of a strong leader and a plan to help "the people."[7] In particular, Liberals think that serious problems can be solved only by a powerful federal government headed by a benevolent Liberal with a bold new plan devised by a few talented and caring people. This authoritarian idea has powered much of the politics of the Democratic party since 1932.

The "strong president" Democrat Franklin Roosevelt had a bold plan, "The New Deal," which among other things took care of the elderly through Social Security. President Lyndon Johnson's plan gave us "The Great Society" which sought to take care of poor people. President William Clinton tried to complete the Liberal welfare state with his bold new health care plan to take care of the sick. This ancient idea has a lot of appeal to people in the Liberal community, the university, the government and the press.

Such perceptions, in my Libertarian opinion, are more suitable to the small principalities of a feudalistic time than to a superpower moving into the information age of the 21st century. In feudal times one could think about politics and economics in simple terms. For instance, one could think of wealth as a relatively fixed quantity to be cut up as a pie, with the largest share distributed to the governing elite, of course. Citizens who were mostly farmers, could be thought of as ignorant peasants unable to do much more than raise grain and children. Thus, these helpless peasants needed a strong and caring lord to rule over them. Liberals buy into this authoritarian way of understanding society.

Authoritarian Liberalism often flies under the flag of "social responsibility." Liberals think they have a social responsibility to care for those who can't care for themselves and to one degree or another, that includes most of us. Thus, Liberals require power over the people in order to exercise their responsibility to help them.

←——— less government	more government ———→
Libertarians **Conservatives**	**Liberals** **Socialists**

THE AUTHORITIAN SCALE

The old political scale with socialists on one end and fascists on the other is not accurate. The socialists, fascists and the social democrats of Europe as well as the Liberals of America all favor a strong central government for what they see as the betterment of society. It makes sense to put all these big government people at the same end of the political spectrum. Conservatives want less government influence on the lives of citizens. Libertarians want the least.

It is important to note that the same words have different meaning to the various ideological camps. When Liberals talk about freedom they mean *freedom from* the effects of bad things. They speak of freedom from want, freedom from sickness, freedom from unemployment. This is part of the same authoritarian tendency, because these are "freedoms" that only the *authority* of big government can supply. In other words, it is the authority of the Liberal welfare state that supplies our freedoms.

This style of thinking can be seen in political reporting. For instance the press routinely accuses Republicans of not being serious about education, because they don't have a plan for the government to implement a new costly program. In the 1988 presidential campaign, candidate George Bush vowed to become the education president. And on April 18, 1991, President George Bush announced his plan for education. The responses from Democrats and the press were predictable. Liberal Democrats criticized the President for not proposing an infusion of federal money into the educational system.

This same attitude was reflected in the evening news. I don't mean that journalists simply reported that Democrats were calling for more money for education. I mean that journalists told the public that education should get more money. Every broadcast that day led off the evening news with the education story. And the message from ABC, NBC, CBS and CNN was "if the President is really serious about education, he needs to propose more federal money for education."

Like their socialist cousins, political Liberals perceive a dark side to capitalism, which tends to oppress the poor. They see capitalism as a good system but one which need to be made responsible and sensitive to "human needs and rights." They think that the government should take care of those who do not do well in the capitalistic system. For instance, 68 percent of the media elite think that the government should reduce the income gap and 48 percent think that the government should guarantee jobs.[8] I take this to mean that most elite journalists favor some form of welfare state funded by a more benevolent kind of capitalism. A colorful and revealing example of this attitude is seen in a commentary by the late journalist John Chancellor of NBC News.

EXAMPLE: John Chancellor's Commentary

In my opinion the attitude of elite journalists was most cogently expressed by Mr. John Chancellor on June 11, 1991 in his commentary on the *NBC Nightly News*. "The quality of life in most of Western Europe is good and improving. And you ask yourself why they have fewer problems than we do. They're capitalist countries. So is the United States. What's is the difference? One difference, I think, is that Western Europe handles its capitalism differently. Western Europe practices a flexible kind of managed capitalism instead of the hands-off Daddy Warbucks kind we say we practice. But that may be changing. Odd things are happening in the United States. Did you ever think the American Medical Association would call for a complete overhaul of national health care? That Ronald Reagan would endorse national gun control. That President Bush would propose national standards for educational testing. All these national ideas are in effect today in the countries of Western Europe. They are part of Europe's system of managed capitalism. These prosperous and competitive Europeans aren't spinning their wheels arguing about gun control, flag burning, health care or abortion. The Europeans spend their time on education and competitiveness and long-range strategies for energy conservation. What makes countries like Germany so competitive, and so rich, is that they've developed a twentieth century model of capitalism while Americans seem to be driving the old nineteenth century model. Some experts say, the United States has only ten years left, if it's going to stay competitive."

The ideal of a (socially) *responsible capitalism* is fairly widespread in the press. It is articulated by Professor Herbert Gans in his studies of the news. "The underlying posture of the news toward the economy resembles that taken toward the polity: an optimistic faith that in the good society, businessmen and women will compete with each other in order to create increased prosperity for all, but that they will refrain from unreasonable profits and gross exploitation of workers of customers." Dr. Gans goes on to state that journalists believe that government also has a role. "Domestic news has by now acknowledged the necessity for the welfare state; even in the good society, the market cannot do everything."[9]

THE COLD WAR WAS NOT WORTH FIGHTING

In 1917, political extremists seized power in Russia. Known as *Communists*, they spent the next 20 years consolidating a dictatorship that sought to control every aspect of Russian life. The same notion of total government control arose in Germany under the National Socialists, known as Nazis. For Nazi and Communist bureaucrats genocide was a routine government activity like issuing drivers licenses and dispensing heath care. Both shared an intense political hatred of those who might resist the power of the state. People with anti-government views were considered to be vermin, to be exterminated like any other pest. The reign of terror that ensued in Russia and Germany took millions lives.

There is every reason to believe that the Communists who ran Russia were going to deal with the rest of the world with the same cold political hate they had displayed at home. However, the western democracies, especially the United States stood in their way. Russian Communists could not defeat the United States in traditional high intensity warfare. Thus, they sought every opportunity to diminish the political power of the United States by using the techniques of propaganda, subversion, and low intensity warfare. This Communist threat and the measures taken to counter it, between 1917 and 1990, is what I am calling the Cold War. It should be noted that most start the Cold War at the end of World War Two. I claim that conflict was built into Communist ideology from the beginning and as soon as they gained political power, the war was on.

During World War Two both Liberals and Conservatives sought the unconditional defeat of German Fascism. However, during the Cold War few Liberals and all Conservatives sought the defeat of Communism. In general, Liberals did not perceive any real danger from Communism. The more radical Liberals perceived Communism as a hope, if flawed, to poor people everywhere. To one degree or another, Liberals wanted to reach an accommodation with the Communists. As most liberals saw it, if there was any danger to democracy, it was from American Conservatives.

This "no danger from the Communists" attitude dominated the reporting on the Cold War. Journalists often referred to a "superpower competition between East and West," as if the Soviet Union were, perhaps, misguided but relatively benign. Or journalists might refer to a "mistrust" between the Soviet Union and America. This language makes a kind of moral equivalence between democratic America and totalitarian Communist Russia.

Now the Cold War with Russian Communists is over and the democracies have won. Casualties were incredibly high. Tens of millions of people perished in government engineered famines, death camps and killing fields. But, news of Communist genocide did not shake old Cold War perceptions of many Liberal journalists. They continue to tell news consumers that there was no real danger from the spread of Communism, that democratic America and Communist Soviet Union were morally equivalent and shared responsibility for causing the Cold War!

EXAMPLE: CNN's Cold War

In the winter of 1998 - 1999, CNN aired a twenty-five-part program purporting to be a history of the Cold War. The old Liberal idea of moral equivalence and American culpability dominated the series. Consider this from the thirteenth in that series titled, "Defining Moments," which aired on January 3, 1999.

Consider this from the narrator Kenneth Branagh, "The Marshal Plan set out to build a European consumer society. The United States wanted a free enterprise western block, peaceful, united and tied to American trade and capital. The Soviet Union was forced to build its own rival block. The people of the socialist countries would eye the west for forty years."

This stuff leaves me breathless. Branagh actually suggests here that it was the United States who really started the Cold War. And he further suggests that America was primarily interested in opening new markets. A kind of capitalistic imperialism. Branagh says the Soviet Union was "forced to respond" as if the Communists were responding to American threats and it was perfectly reasonable for the Soviet Union to enslave all of Eastern Europe.

From host Ralph Beglighter: "As the Cold War intensified both sides feared betrayal from enemies at home. In the United States, the hunt for spies and Communists was conducted by the House Committee on Un-American Activities. It investigated the State Department, many other government agencies and Hollywood. ... As the McCarthy Hearing spread fear and suspicion across the United States, several KGB agents and spies were uncovered by the FBI and convicted. In the Soviet Union, Stalin feared traitors were everywhere. Party loyalty was enforced by his iron will and the police state."

Beglighter suggests a moral equivalence by linguistly treating McCarthy and Stalin the same. "Both sides feared betrayal at home." Equating Senator McCarthy who was a demagogue at worst and Stalin who killed a few million of his own people at best, is a characteristic way to make the equivalence.

While the threat of all out nuclear war with Russian Communists has passed, the Cold War is not yet over. The world's largest country, China, is still ruled by the same goose stepping Communist party that saw millions to their death during the great cultural revolution in the 1960s. It is as if the Nazi party which perpetrated the Holocaust in the 1940s were still governing Germany today. North Korea and Cuba are still run by the same thugs spawned by Russian Communists. And many in the American press are still suggesting that there is not now nor has there ever been any real danger to anyone from these folks.

JEWS OCCUPY ISRAEL AND OPPRESS ARABS

In 1947 the United Nations portioned the area called Palestine into Jewish and Arab sectors. However, the Arabs wanted all the land. Surrounding Arab states declared war on Israel from the very moment it became a state in 1948. While that war is complex and nuanced, it continues to this day. And the coverage of the Cold War informs analysis of the coverage of Arab/Israeli conflicts.

The press covers the Arab threat to Israel as they covered the Communist threat to the western democracies, as if it only existed in the paranoia of the right wing government. The elite press reports on the state of Israel as if Jews were an occupying army that took the land away from its rightful owners, the so-called Palestinian arabs. Jews are portrayed as brutes using excessive power against helpless and hapless Palestine Arabs.

THERE IS NO RIGHT TO OWN A FIREARM

Judging by the evening news, elite journalists don't believe that people have a fundamental right to own a rifle let alone "bear arms." The press portrays people who defend themselves as "vigilantes." News consumers are told that those people are political zealots who pose a real danger to society. You don't need a PhD in sociology to observe that most journalists oppose the private ownership of firearms. Just watch the way the press covers the issue.

Journalists frame the ownership issue as one of *"gun control,"* putting it in the category of controlling commodities like drugs or nuclear waste. That's the Liberal position. Thus "gun control" is a loaded phrase. It assumes that ownership of guns should be controlled by the government like dangerous substances. People who believe they have a fundamental right to own a firearm are referred as "gun enthusiasts." This demeaning label belittles people who claim fundamental rights of firearm ownership. (It would be a little like calling feminists who fight for equality in the workplace, "career enthusiasts.") By using the "gun control" characterization, journalists assume that the Liberal side is correct and the Conservative side is wrong.

Story selection also favors anti-gun bias. The press is interested only in showing the harm that gun ownership can bring. Thus, news of the victims of gun-toting criminals gets a big play. Over the last ten years, the evening news has presented an endless flow of news stories about "the victims of gun violence." At the same time the press is not very interested in showing the benefits of gun ownership. Stories of people who successfully defend themselves with firearms are back-paged or ignored altogether. And when such stories make the news, journalists tend to paint them as vigilantes who are more dangerous than the criminals.

The texture of these news stories demonstrates the downside of the private ownership of firearms. Journalists are fond of showing us lots of blood in their coverage. "If it bleeds, it leads!" Journalists tell us that's just the way the news business works. They tell us that there is news value to the bloody side of gun ownership. That may be true. But this "neutral" news judgement seems to evaporate when the same journalists get to the abortion issue. The bloody side of abortion seems to have no news value. We never see the dismembered body of a destroyed "fetus."

HOWEVER, WOMEN HAVE A RIGHT TO ABORTION

The Liberal press only deems the benefits of abortion to be newsworthy. Elite journalists have no interest in the downside of unlimited abortion rights. Instead they seek out news stories which suggest that it is good for women to have unlimited access to abortion. News stories which might bring this "right" into question are avoided. People (including journalists) have a natural aversion for information which is inconsistent with their way of thinking.

That's because abortion benefits stories are consistent with the political beliefs of most journalists. They strongly favor the idea that a woman has a fundamental constitutional right to an abortion.[10] Even without academic studies, one need only take a casual look at the coverage of the issue to conclude that the press favors the Liberal position on the issue. Like the coverage of most political issues, news stories are severely one-sided.

One-sidedness is characteristic of bias. News stories on political issues are reported exclusively from the Liberal point of view. Competing Libertarian, Conservative and Populist perspectives are often treated as strange, foreign and illegitimate. *Knowledge of Liberals' ideas can be used to predict the coverage of political disputes.* For instance, knowing that Liberals have socialist tendencies explains the very favorable coverage of Democratic President Clinton's attempt to orchestrate the delivery of health care from Washington. In general, the press tells news consumers that Liberal opinion is proven fact.

THE ENVIRONMENTALISTS ARE RIGHT

Another victim of capitalism, from the Liberal point of view, is the environment. The idea here is that capitalists trample the environment in a greedy pursuit of unearned profits. Most journalists are sympathetic to the various issues of the environmental movement, global warming, allocation of renewable resources, the use of public lands, etc. Only 19 percent of elite journalists think that environmental problems are overstated.[11]

For instance, if you watch the evening news, you would get the idea that man-made global warming is proven scientific fact to which all scientists adhere and that the forests of the northeast have been destroyed by acid rain. Neither is a proven scientific fact, yet the press continues to report these fictions as if they were fact.

Environmental reporting results from the cozy relationship between the Liberal press and Liberal interest groups. They have a symbiotic relationship. Journalists trust the "facts" supplied to them by Liberal interest groups. And Liberal interest groups trust the mainstream press to find a way to get their public relations messages into the news free of charge. The press coverage of "events" staged by Liberal interest groups brings up an important question.

If the press refused to cover a political demonstration, would it happen? That is, if the demonstrators could not get a little free air on the nightly news for their partisan message, would they even show up? Not likely. Interest groups trying to influence public opinion will stage "events" to promote their political cause or commercial product. The elite press will find a way to provide a convenient sounding board for Liberal interest groups.

A SMALL CONSERVATIVE VOICE

Liberal ideas still dominate the center of the news, that is, the front pages of the elite press. As of this writing, nearly all the Non-Liberal news is found at the margins of the news, that is, the back pages, some news talk shows, C-SPAN and one-time news stories. Non-Liberal news sometimes appears at the center of the news, but it does not stay there long. And the Liberal press goes on with its work as if the non-Liberal facts were never aired.

Conservatives know that their perspective is shut out of the mass media. Conservatives know they are the butt of nearly all the political humor that emanates from Hollywood. As already noted, a review of PBS documentaries displayed a definite tilt favoring Liberal opinion. PBS documentaries have not presented a diversity of views and their coverage of issues is also one-sided.[12] For years the elite news has been tailored for the consumption of Liberal news consumers. Information required by Liberal voters has always been readily available.

However, political Liberals likely comprise no more than twenty percent of the population. This means that there was an unfulfilled information demand in the mass media. Conservative, Libertarian and Populist voters had to proactively search the margins of the news to get useful information. Elite news organizations let the demand for non-Liberal information go begging. Only insular journalists of the Liberal press were surprised (and alarmed), when Rush Limbaugh and other radio talk show commentators tried to fill that demand. Talk radio has become a conduit for information of use to Conservatives.

If there were some sort of political diversity in the newsroom, non-Liberal voters would not have sought a channel around the Liberal press. While talk radio meets some of the demand for fact-based editorial news, the demand for daily objective reporting is still largely unfilled. The 24-hour Fox News Network may be moving into that news vacuum.

The rise of technology also helped bypass the Liberal gatekeepers. The Cable Satellite Public Affairs Network (C-SPAN), provides news consumers with easy access to events such as sessions of Congress, various government and political meetings, in their entirety! This gives news consumers the opportunity to evaluate events for themselves. Another technological development works against the traditional gatekeepers. News information flows through the Internet. People have easy access to documents public and private, previous newspaper stories and a profusion of information and data. It is now easier for news consumers to get information that the elite press conveniently leaves out.

SUMMARY

What I have presented here are some of the ideas which animate the Liberal vision of the world. The welfare state is good for you. Man-made global warming and acid rain are proven scientific facts. Nuclear power is a bad idea. The Cold War was an ignoble cause. There is no fundamental right to "bear arms." And poverty causes crime. Whether journalists choose to call themselves Liberal or not, this set of ideas is part of what is commonly called Liberal ideology.[13] This partisan body of ideas is the background upon which the news is painted.

The essence of Liberal ideological bias in the news is that, *leading journalists will find a way to tell news consumers that Liberal ideas are proven fact. Journalists use Liberal opinion to explain news events.*

While there is a growing alternate media -- Matt Drudge, Rush Limbaugh, talk radio, C-SPAN and the Internet -- the partisan Liberal gatekeepers still dominate the mass media. There is little diversity in the brand name news organizations. One way or another, the same old Liberal ideas dominate the news at the expense of competing points of view. In fact, Liberal ideas resonate throughout the whole Liberal media from fictitious journalist Murphy Brown to actual journalist Dan Rather. The evening news is what the world looks like through the eyes of a Liberal Democrat.

DISCUSSION

I have relied heavily on the studies of Lichter, Rothman and Lichter in characterizing elite journalists as dominantly Liberal. I consider their study of the elite journalists to be compelling. Lichter and team did not simply ask journalists where they place themselves on a left/right political spectrum as other studies have done. The problem with simply asking a journalist where he places himself is that one man's Liberal is another man's middle-of-the-roader. And journalists trying to fend off accusations of Liberal bias have motivation to misrepresent their political leanings, claiming to be moderate or independent.

The Lichter studies use a sound methodology for discovering the worldview of leading journalists. The Lichter team polled elite journalists on their voting habits and found that they voted overwhelmingly for the Democrat for President. They sought to discover how journalists felt on specific issues like economics, the environment and nuclear energy. They looked at the profile of journalists. The Lichter team used the Thematic Appreciation Test to provide some insight into the motivations of leading journalists. These results were published in a book, *The Media Elite*, by Robert Lichter, Stanley Rothman and Linda Lichter. That 1987 book established the fact that leading journalists are political Liberals.

This leaves the question, does the Liberal attitude of the elite press influence the news products they produce? The work of Lichter and associates aside, most other academics claim that there is no ideological bias in the news. Consider Professor Michael Robinson, who studies the press. He is a self-identified political Liberal. He studied the 1984 presidential election and published his results in *Public Opinion* magazine. He and his team studied 826 news pieces. When addressing the question of "issue bias," they found "only 2.5 percent of all the pieces implied a liberal position *or* a conservative position on any issued discussed in the piece."

Professor Robinson claimed that only 11 out of the 826 pieces contained any Liberal point of view or 1.3 percent. He asserted that this "is hardly enough to move an electorate --- even a liberal electorate. More important, the majority of those twenty-one pieces that showed bias were *commentaries*, the appropriate place for policy opinion." What Professor Robinson is saying here is that there was less than one percent issue bias in the content of the news and that was not enough to influence public opinion.[14]

I dispute that conclusion. First, there is a perception problem. When a Conservative watches the evening news, he does not perceive the truth. He hears a Liberal voice and concludes the news is biased. This is important. Conservatives and Liberals don't experience their differences as one of ideas (ideology). Liberals and Conservatives differ over what is true about the world. When a Liberal academic watches the evening news,` he likely hears what he thinks is mostly the truth, contaminated only by the greed of people who own the news networks. Liberal academics will likely have difficulty perceiving any Liberal bias in the news. Therefore, it is not surprising they fail to find it.

Secondly, a propagandist could tell you that an expert selection of the truth is the very best propaganda. Thus, the fact that Professor Robinson found little explicitly stated ideological bias in the text of news reports does not imply the absence of *significant* Liberal bias. What about the use of ideologically loaded labels like "anti-abortionist" and "gun control?" What about politically one-sided news selection in the coverage of ideologically based issues? What about using Liberal ideas to explain people and events? These more subtle aspects of news production can produce significant ideological bias.

But most importantly, *few people talk in explicitly ideological terms*. Even politicians rarely utter anything explicitly ideological. A

Liberal politician does not say, "I favor socialized medicine." He says something like, "I favor the 'single payer plan' for solving the looming health care crisis." It is my observation that people view their own ideology not as ideas, but as the simple truth. For instance, journalists may not think of themselves as a Liberals, but simply good people with a *social conscience* who have a *social responsibility* to help the "little guy and gal." Nationalizing health care, providing more welfare benefits, ensuring "gun control" and a woman's fundamental "right to an abortion" is the way to do that. And, of course, a powerful federal government is required to accomplish these worthy tasks.

END NOTES

(1) Lichter, S. Robert, and others. **The Media Elite**. Bethesda, Maryland: Adler & Adler Publishers Inc., 1986. page 132.

(2) By leading journalists I refer to the major dailies, *The New York Times*, *The Wall Street Journal*, *The Washington Post* and *The Los Angeles Times*; the weekly news magazines: *Time*, *Newsweek* and *U.S.News & World Report*; the television networks: The American Broadcasting Company (ABC), The National Broadcasting Company (NBC), The Columbia Broadcasting System (CBS) as well as The Public Broadcasting Service (PBS) and The Cable News Network (CNN).

(3) See CNBC's "Hardball" for July 5, 1996, hosted by Chris Matthews.

(4) Partisans often use the word "ideology" as an epithet. This meaning of the word ideology implies *a simplistic body of stupid ideas ineptly applied by "ideologues" to solve problems they know nothing about.*

(5) See a Close Up Foundation program which aired on C-SPAN in 1986. In a talk to students, ABC Correspondent Ann Compton was asked, "A majority of people believe the press too often tends to favor one side in its coverage of issues. A plurality suggests there is often political bias. [sic] What do you think?" She answered, "I say no to the political bias. ... It is not a matter of preference of the

reporters of which candidate is the one they favor. ... It's not a political influence. In terms of how we cover the national scene, and the national presidential campaigns, I think it's true that we tend to take, ... we tend to go into issues stories with kind of a preconceived idea that one side of the issue is the logical right one or the logical wrong one. ... We go in with the kind of thinking, this hearing or news event is going to prove one side of the case or the other. But, ... we often throw in the dissenting voice. ... Yes we do go in with a preconceived idea on some issues. But it's not a question of political bias. And it's not even a question of Liberal versus Conservative. It's an issue of what is generally accepted right or wrong." Close Up Foundation, 1235 Jefferson Davis Highway, Arlington, VA 22202; (800)-368-5400.

(6) See pages 221, 222 of **Good Intentions Make Bad News** by S. Robert Lichter and Richard E. Noyes, published by Rowman & Littlefield Publishers, Inc., in Lanham, Maryland, in 1995.

(7) See the article by John Gray titled, Utopian Academics and the Collapse of Communism, starting on page 66 of *Academic Questions*, winter 1991 92 Volume 5 Number 1, Transaction Periodicals Consortium, New Brunswick, N.J.

(8) See **The Media Elite**, page 29, table 2.

(9) See pages 46-47 of **Deciding What's News** by Herbert J. Gans, New York, Pantheon Books, 1979.

(10) See page 29, table 2 of **The Media Elite**.

(11) See page 29, table 2 of **The Media Elite**.

(12) See Balance and Diversity in PBS Documentaries by S. Robert Lichter, Daniel Amundson and Linda S. Lichter. Published by the Center for Media and Public Affairs, in Washington, D.C., in March of 1992

(13) There are comments by journalists themselves on the margins of the news which acknowledge that most journalists are Liberal Democrats. For instance in an article in the *American Journalism*

Review in April 1993, Todd Gitlin said, "But why should reporters, most of the [sic, them?] Democrats in their voting lives, lean harder on Democrats than on their natural nemeses?" And this from Sally Quinn of the *Washington Post*, "Ronald Reagan, I think, had quite a good press and I think part of it even though most journalists didn't really like him or agree with his positions, he was coming right after Watergate and I do think there was this standoff and we can't be seen to be these Liberals who are always out to get all Republicans or Conservatives."

(14) See page 36 of **The Mass Media in Campaign '84** edited by Michael J. Robinson and Austin Ranney, published by the American Enterprise Institute in Washington D.C., in 1985.

Chapter 5

POLITICAL FAVORITISM

Prejudice is a way of thinking. When people act on their prejudices, the result is called discrimination. When people act on their racial prejudice, the result is called racial discrimination. When people act on their gender prejudice, it is called gender discrimination. And over time, this behavior settles into various discriminatory practices.

A discriminatory practice is a policy employed by bigots to enforce their prejudice. All forms of discrimination find expression in various practices. Consider racial discrimination. Up until the 1950s, racial bigots made it a practice to prevent African-Americans from getting service in restaurants, loans from banks and rooms in hotels. African-Americans had trouble getting jobs. Businesses found excuses to deny them employment, even when there were job openings. African-Americans were treated as second class citizens. There was one set of rules for the majority in-group and another set of rules for the minority out-group. There was a double standard.

When journalists act on their political prejudices, I call the result political *favoritism*. Political favoritism in the press follows the same general outline as other forms of discrimination. Press favoritism has its roots in the prejudices and stereotypes common to political Liberals. Journalists tend to glorify Liberal Democrats and denigrate Conservative Republicans. Journalists insist that their Liberal ideas get a very fair hearing, while treating Conservative ideas with scorn. (Note that a Conservative press would indulge in its own brand of favoritism. However, as of this writing, Liberals still dominate the media show from Hollywood to Public Broadcasting to television and the evening news.) The routine favoritism practices of the press establishment define a partisan double standard.

A PARTISAN DOUBLE STANDARD

The double standard in the news is obvious. During the 1994 off-year Congressional campaign, the press told us that soccer moms voted for Democrats, while angry white men voted for Republicans. If a Democrat suddenly adopts a Republican position on some issue of the day, the press tells us that he cleverly "co-opted the issue." If a Republican adopts a Democratic position on an issue, he is said to "flip-flop." If an audience likes what a Democratic speaker had to say, the press tells that he "excited the crowd." If people like what a Republican had to say, he is said to have "pressed hot buttons."

Liberal journalists tell us that Democrats only have a few little character flaws, while Republicans are serious wrongdoers. Or as Correspondent Brit Hume said on *This Week with David Brinkley* (August 23, 1994), "When the Democrats play rough and tumble politics like the Republicans have done in the past, we all say, 'See they really want to win and how smart it is.' And when the Republicans do it, we all say it's dirty politics, negative campaigning and we should disapprove of it."

These tendentious evaluations of Republicans and Democrats seen on the evening news mimic the partisan stereotypes common to political Liberals. Let me review. Republicans are seen as fundamentally insensitive, selfish people unfit for high political office. However, Democrats are seen as fundamentally good people making them the natural inheritors of political power. Of course, Republicans may occasionally do something good and Democrats may occasionally do something bad, but the stereotypes still hold.

For instance, the type of criticism journalists lodge against the two major political parties illustrates the partisan double standard. Journalists deny such charges, of course. They claim to give Democrats and Republicans equally bad press. They tell us that the negative press they submit to Democrats is equivalent to the hostile press they fire at Republicans. The actual volume of criticism in seconds of television time or lines of print allocated to Republicans and Democrats may be equal. However, press *criticism of Republicans is qualitatively different from criticism of Democrats.*

Examples abound. Consider the comments of Bryant Gumbel, formerly of NBC's *Today Show* and now with CBS. He referred to political lies of a particular sort as "Republicanesque." Or consider the way the press remembers the 1988 presidential election. It has been widely reported that Republican George Bush had cynically used race to be elected. And every day during the Republican national convention of 1992, some television journalist accused some Republican of being some sort of racist. After the Republicans won the 1994 off-year election, the Liberal press acquired another target, Speaker of the House Newt Gingrich. He has been characterized as selfish and mean "Scrooge" and "Grinch."

In contrast, the press criticism submitted to leading Democrats is of a kinder and gentler sort. This criticism presupposes that Democrats are good people who should be praised for what they are trying to do. At worst Democrats only fall down on the job. The press would have news consumers believe that leading Democrats don't have serious ethical lapses or engage in wrongdoing. And if they ever actually do any of these things, it's not important, because Democrats do so much good for so many people. Journalists tell us to discount the faults of Democrats. And even though journalists may put a little edge to their criticism of Democrats, it's still a form of *constructive criticism.* When compared to the destructive criticism laid on leading Republicans, it amounts to a false kind of criticism.[1]

The news of leading Democrats looks and sounds different than news of leading Republicans. News stories of Democrats often resemble public service announcements while the news of Republicans often has an aggressive critical edge to it. News about Democrats is evaluated according to one journalistic standard, while news about Republicans is evaluated according to a very different journalistic standard. Elite news organizations cover Democrats with a helpful public spirited brand of journalism. I call that way of doing news business, *flack journalism.* In contrast, most elite news organizations act as an opposition press to Republicans. I call that, *attack journalism.* This partisan double standard is such an integral part of the cultural fabric of the press establishment that journalists hardly seem to even notice it.

ATTACK JOURNALISM

When covering Republicans and Conservatives, most journalists don their "watchdog" hat. They assume the stance of a defender of the public good. Claiming that there is a natural adversarial relationship between the press and politicians, journalists act as if they have a constitutional mandate to provide a counterpoint to public officials. Journalists claim that it is their job to "hold politicians' feet to the fire" because the American people have a "right to know" what their leaders are doing. Journalists claim it is a routine part of their job to ask "the hard question." This attack journalism ranges from nit-picking news reports to outright verbal attacks. First, let's look at the nit-picking attack.

It is ridiculously easy for journalists to make a Republican target appear incompetent. Simply spotlight his mistakes and missteps. Lead news consumers to believe that these gaffes are the tip of an iceberg of unfitness. I call this favoritism practice "the partisan gaffe watch." It works like this: (1) downplay anything of substance the target Republican says; (2) give disproportionate coverage to verbal errors; (3) Find ways to suggest that the frequent gaffes imply incompetence; and then (4) turn around and blame the Republican for the gaffes, noting that he "keeps stepping in it." The four-year gaffe watch on Republican Vice President Dan Quayle provides a good example.

When Republican presidential candidate George Bush chose Senator Dan Quayle to be his running mate in August of 1988, the media elite reflexively judged Senator Quayle to be unfit for high office and set out to prove it. The national press corps dispatched a couple of thousand journalists to Quayle's home state of Indiana to dig for political dirt. They did this under the guise of providing public information on an unknown candidate. Senator Quayle's whole adult life, including his draft status during the Vietnam War, was fair game. This "feeding frenzy," turned up little, but the lack of facts did little to prevent continuing press attacks on Quayle.[2]

Since journalists could not attack Quayle directly, they resorted to an indirect attack, the partisan gaffe watch. The elite media ignored whatever Quayle said of any substance and simply waited for the inevitable verbal gaffes. On a routine basis journalists used the gaffes to suggest that Quayle was an incompetent buffoon. After four years of nit-picking journalism, Vice President Quayle's reputation was in tatters. The press was unable to knock him off with a single stroke. It was, however, a political death by a thousand pricks.

Journalists claim they are fair and balanced. But a fair and balanced presentation of Quayle's "gaffes" is neither fair nor balanced. If journalists hunted gaffes regardless of who committed the gaffe, they would surely have happened upon those of President Clinton. For instance he said in a televised interview on November 2, 1992 that, "African-Americans watch the same news at night that *ordinary Americans* [emphasis added]. If there is, there is an overwhelming bias in what they see, based on conflict, failure, process, politics and negativism, as opposed to just giving the people the facts about what's going on ... [sic] Then they, ... You can't expect people to vote on what they don't know." Suggesting that African-Americans are not ordinary people sounds racist by the standard used on Republicans. Surely this was a serious gaffe.

The truth is that everybody makes verbal gaffes. We all say dumb things from time to time. We all say things we wish we had not. We all have foibles; it is a condition of being human. The reality is that a hostile gaffe watch could have made the absentminded Albert Einstein look like an idiot. The fact that any reporter can gather a bag of gaffes made by a public figure is meaningless. It's like catching a man using the men's room. That's not news, unless he is using a toilet as a mail drop to his Chinese Communist case officer.

Another favoritism practice is *the attack interview*. In what amounts to a contact sport, Liberal Journalists ask questions calculated to embarrass or trip up a Republican target. And for some journalists it is a blood sport, especially during public relations battles between Republicans and Democrats. They may try for that killer question that will lead people to believe that the Republican target is totally unfit for public office.

A case in point was the confrontation between CBS anchor Dan Rather and Vice President George Bush on the evening news in 1988. Bush was running for president on the Republican ticket. For the entire interview, some several minutes long, Rather badgered Vice President Bush, trying to get him to confess to alleged involvement in the Iran/Contra Scandal.[3] Bush claimed to be "out of the loop" and not involved in any scandalous activity.

Mr. Rather flatly refused to accept that answer, told the audience so, and pressed on with a mulish sequence of accusatory questions.

FLACK JOURNALISM

Journalists undergo a spectacular attitude change when they cover Democrats. In the presence of Democrats, journalists are at their ease. A friendly bantering sense of humor surfaces. (Contrast the daily briefings of the Clinton White House with the briefings given by the Reagan or Bush White Houses.) Journalists are loath to ask hard questions. And they never badger a leading Democrat with a steady stream of attack questions as Dan Rather did to Republican George Bush.

When covering Democrats the definition of good journalism also undergoes change. Gone is the drive to provide a counterpoint to slippery politicians entrenched in their positions of power and privilege. Journalists suddenly find that they have a responsibility to keep citizens well informed about the public policies proposed by the Democrats. That is, many elite journalists become "flacks" for the welfare state and the Democratic party.

According to the *Associated Press Stylebook*, "flack" is slang for press agent. A press agent is a promoter whose job it is to put a positive spin on information about his client. A press agent: (1) tells people that his client is a good person, (2) brags about his great accomplishments, (3) amplifies good news when it happens, and (4) tries to minimize the damage of bad news. In other words, the primary task of a flack to protect and glamorize his boss. The object is to make the boss popular.

That is exactly what the Liberal press does for leading Democrats, glamorize them.[4] Even though journalists restrain themselves somewhat, in order to maintain their credibility, there is still more than enough wiggle room to help improve the public opinion ratings of leading Democrats. I suspect that journalists experience the behavior differently. They likely see themselves as merely trying making the world a better place.

Likely journalists view their flacking activities as performing a public service. In any case, the Liberal press functions as if it were its job to educate the public about the welfare state. It airs these partisan promotions as if presenting public service announcements. The press has been performing this sort of "public service" since the advent of the welfare state during the presidency of Franklin Roosevelt.

During the 1930s working journalists were very supportive of President Roosevelt and his so-called "New Deal" for America. "Most reporters, like most Americans, were sympathetic to the New Deal program. But ideological affinity and personal sympathy for the President did not solely account for the [Roosevelt] administrations's popularity with the press. Rather, it was the ability of the White House to provide a steady supply of readily available news and information."[5]

The central theme of the New Deal was that capitalism needed to be reformed and the "New Deal" welfare state was exactly the instrument to achieve that reform. The first installment of that reform was Social Security, which became law during the New Deal years of the 1930s. Later, in the 1960s, Democratic President Lyndon Johnson installed a number of federal programs designed to fight poverty. It was called, "The War on Poverty." And the 1992 election of Democrat William Clinton to the presidency brought the promise of government-supplied health care. The federal government would take care of the elderly, the poor and the sick.

The promise of a complete welfare state headed by a "good man," William Clinton, energized the Liberal press after the 1992 presidential election. Between inauguration day in 1993 and the death of the Clinton Health Care Plan in 1994, there was a lot of cheerleading for the Democrats. The Liberal press covered the health care issue as if there were a national consensus that Liberal ideas were true and correct. Story after story on the evening news featured health care issues and told us that nationalizing much of the delivery of health care was the humane thing to do. Today's journalists helped Democrats get their health care message out much as yesterday's journalists did for the New Deal programs of the 1930s.

Flacking news stories exhibit distinguishing characteristics. With an air of doing a public service, journalists tell us that: (1) Mr. Leading Democrat is a good person; (2) who is trying to doing good things and (3) we should admire him for it. Consider this Tom Brokaw lead to an *NBC Nightly News* story of January 22, 1993 titled "Fighting Back." "Too many American young people are being robbed of their childhood by the growing violence in our society. Bill and Hillary Clinton are determined to change that. But as NBC's Mike Vetcher shows us tonight, it's possible but not easy." (Mr. Vetcher went on to present the news story.) This lead implies that the Clintons are good people and suggests that we should admire them.

Interviews provide another format for flacking messages seemingly designed to help leading Democrats. These interviews are a conspicuous contrast to the attack interviews used on Republicans. Flacking interviews are characterized by softball questions and friendly chitchat in an environment sympathetic to the leading Democratic politician. Democrats are treated with respect and courtesy. They are given plenty of time, without tendentious interruption, to deliver their partisan messages to a mass audience. Interview questions are helpful. In general, journalists want to know how the Democrats are going to implement their good programs and defeat those nasty Republicans. Embedded in these questions are cheerleading messages like: "This is a good guy;" "He has good motives;" "He does good deeds;" and "You should admire him." Yes, there may be a hard question or two, but such questions are asked in a *pro forma* fashion without serious follow-up. Thus, flacking interviews are not much more than infomercials that sell the political products of Liberal Democrats.

EXAMPLE: Rather and Clinton

A good example of these sweetheart interviews is one that CBS's Sixty Minutes did with President Clinton that aired August 18, 1996, shortly after the 1996 Republican national convention. During that convention, some Republicans had leveled criticism at Democrat Clinton. CBS gave President Clinton what amounted to free airtime to attack Republicans. Correspondent Morley Safer set up the interview with this amazingly partisan statement, "It has been a long time since one political party jumped on, really stomped on a sitting president as the Republicans did last week in San Diego. This afternoon Dan Rather sat down with President Clinton, in the White House, and looked at the rough week that was."

Safer needed only to go back to the 1992 Democratic convention for stomping on a sitting president. Consider this from a speech by Democratic Senator William Bradley, "The evidence that this administration [of Republican George Bush] inflames the wounds they should heal is everywhere. The spectacle of social crisis that can be seen right through the windows of the White House does not seem to trouble our leader's sleep. They lead the most idealistic nation in history but they are themselves without idealism. Fear, division, and the death of hope, these are the fruits of Republican rule. And so I say to our President this election year, your slogans that camouflage callousness and glamorize greed will profit you nothing." This was not the only example of partisan hate at the 1992 Democratic national convention.

The interview followed the usual flacking format. Dan Rather's tone with President Clinton was friendly and respectful. Rather asked softball questions and gave Clinton plenty of uninterrupted time to answer and pontificate. Rather started the interview with a couple of leading questions: (1) Is Bob Dole too old? (Remember that Senator Bob Dole was the Republican candidate for president) and (2) Has Bob Dole been captured by Republican extremist like Newt Gingrich? (Notice that Rather's question echoed the Democratic canard that many Republicans are extremists.) Journalist Rather then played a video of criticism aimed at the President from the Republican national convention. Clinton was given ample opportunity to answer each criticism. "Are you going to raise taxes?" Clinton answered, "I have no intention to raise taxes." Rather meekly asked one more time and then let the subject drop. When Republicans try to get away with this sort of linguistic dodge, the typical elite journalist will angrily pursue the question, asking it over and over again.

Next, Rather said to the President that the Republicans were going to attack his character. Rather asked the President to comment. Clinton responded by attacking the character of the entire Republican party. Clinton accused Republicans of practicing the politics of personal destruction, noting that Republicans were good at it. Then Clinton turned right around and said that he was not going to make any personal attacks on Republicans. If this hypocrisy bothered Mr. Rather, he did not comment on it.

The partisan double standard is in full force here. The Liberal press treats the hypocrisy of leading Republicans with stern disapproval. The double standard of behavior is the essence of all discrimination including political favoritism. While it is very difficult to modify the prejudiced style of thinking described in earlier chapters, it is relatively easy to modify discriminatory behavior.

The Civil Rights movement of the 1950s and 1960s provides a good illustration. Before the movement, many discriminatory practices were in place. While all of those discriminatory practices have not been completely eliminated, much of the worst behavior has been reduced.

If it is possible to reduce some of the worst of racial discrimination from society, it should be possible to reduce some of the worst of political favoritism in journalism.

However, leading journalists continue to act on their political prejudices. The press establishment still uses the news to influence public opinion, in the name of a "responsibility" to the American people. In practice, that means that the news is produced strictly for the consumption and use of Liberal Democrats. Other political communities - Conservative Republicans, Libertarians and various Populists - are ignored or even attacked by elite journalists. Journalists should stop using the news to achieve the partisan goals and start producing a news of use to a politically pluralistic society.

DISCUSSION

When I began my study of the news, I concentrated on the cognitive processes of reporters. Cognitive biases explained how the unacknowledged Liberal opinions of the vast majority (80 to 90 percent) of elite journalists applied a constant Liberal bias to the news. That's why the evening news is a view of the world through a Liberal window. But as time went by, it became clear to me that the elite press was doing more than painting a Liberal picture of the world. Journalists were doing more than merely expressing their opinions. They were trying to affect political outcomes. They are involved in the process. And I wanted to describe that involvement.

Is all press favoritism deliberate? I think not. Many journalists seem to be unconscious of any legitimate point of view other than the Liberal one. That is, many journalists seem to be unconscious of their prejudices. Others seems to be a bit more conscious. However, I have trouble with the idea of favoritism being largely unconscious. Let me put it this way. I am a Libertarian and often agree with the Liberal point of view. I have no trouble recognizing press bias that agrees with my own thinking. Why can't highly educated, the best of the best, elite journalists do the same? And more importantly I think that journalists are aware that they make Republican and Conservative ideas sit at the back of the media bus.

END NOTES

(1) Edith Efron in her 1972 book, **The News Twisters**, identifies a "false criticism," which she defines as a mild reprimand to a favored political figure which is then followed by enough praise to neutralize the criticism.

(2) The expression "feeding frenzy" comes from the book, **Feeding Frenzy**: How Attack Journalism Has Transformed American Politics by Professor Larry J. Sabato, published by The Free Press, New York in 1991.

(3) See page 198 of **Scandal: The Culture of Mistrust in American Politics** by Suzanne Garment published in New York by Doubleday in 1992 for a description of the scandal.

(4) Edith Efron in her 1971 book, **The News Twisters**, used the expression "glamorizing" to describe the character of the good press given to favored politicians.

(5) See page 13 of Professor Richard W. Steele's book, **Propaganda in an Open Society**: The Roosevelt Administration and the Media, 1933-1941. Westport, Connecticut: Greenwood Press, 1985. Professor Steel also says that reporters often used the story "slant" suggested by President Roosevelt.

The press also cooperated with President Kennedy to manage the news to the benefit of his presidency. Professor Sanford Ungar, Dean, School of Communications, The American University, puts it this way, "I just want to comment on two points. ... Yes, there is something unique about the Reagan administration in recent history. But the truth of the matter is that both in terms of the image of the President with the public and the treatment of the President by the press, the closest parallel is that of John F. Kennedy. And the big difference there is that, when the Kennedy Administration manipulated the news, it did it with the cooperation of the press, instead of the opposition of the press. And everybody was friends and sort of got together after work and talked about what a good job they had done. And in this case the manipulators and manipulatees felt much better about it than we do today. I think that the similarities are great. And we can't forget. It's not that long ago. Somebody said it's been 25 years. I guess it was Hodding who said the idea of managing the news is a 25-year-old concept."

Chapter 6

THE BATTLE FOR PUBLIC OPINION

At the beginning of the twentieth century a group of journalists sought to use the power of mass communication to achieve their political goals. For about ten years, just after the turn of the century, "a group of editors and publishers made common cause with some of the nation's outstanding novelists, poets, historians, lawyers, economists, and researchers. The cause ... was the exposure of the underside of American capitalism." They apparently thought that, "the institutions that controlled the economic and political system were not to be trusted," and should be reformed.[1] This group saw the federal government as the main instrument of change.

The then-President Theodore Roosevelt termed these reformists "muckrakers." Muck is a term for manure or sewage which some unfortunate people at the time had the job of handling with a muck rake. President Roosevelt was saying that these journalists were digging up dirt on people and using it to influence public opinion. Thus, the practice became known as "muckraking" and journalists who did it, "muckrakers." The following flow chart illustrates the muckraking formula.

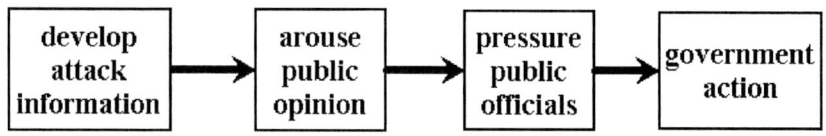

These activist journalists employed a now-familiar technique. Using their investigative capacity, they dug up information about prominent people they considered wrongdoers. They wrote news stories and magazine articles crafted to inflame public opinion against the alleged wrongdoers. They advocated government reforms designed to correct the perceived wrongs. Citizens would then pressure politicians to make changes in law and policy and punish wrongdoers.

Many muckraking journalists thought it was their "social responsibility" to improve American democracy and the plight of the less fortunate. The muckrakers saw themselves as fundamentally good. As H. L. Mencken put it, they only wanted to "comfort the afflicted and afflict the comfortable." It was their self-appointed task to advocate reforms intended to improve working conditions in our flawed American democracy. Those who opposed reforms were seen as selfish Conservatives trying to protect their position of power and privilege. The following figure represents this political landscape.

"CHANGE" versus "STATUS QUO" PARADIGM

GOOD GUYS	BAD GUYS
liberal reformers **promoting "change"**	**privileged conservatives** **protecting the status quo**

This outdated view of politics dominates the elite press and the Liberal wing of the Democratic party. *Their use of the word "change" refers to the implementation of one or more items on the Liberal agenda.* "The Conservatives" who oppose Liberal programs are seen to be in favor of things as they are, the status quo. But this view does not make sense any more. The muckrakers have already won. What was unorthodox in 1900 has become orthodox in 1998. The Liberal agenda, except for nationalizing health care, has been implemented into the Welfare State. Today the Welfare State **is** the status quo! Today, it is powerful Liberals who protect their position of power and privilege in and around the Welfare State. Today correcting the undemocratic excesses of the Welfare State represents real change.

The idea of actively using the news to improve society has grown into a philosophy of journalism some call *social responsibility journalism*.[2] Directed by their *social consciences*, Liberal journalists think they have a responsibility to use the news to improve society and protect the public welfare, as they define it. This means that the news should not be a passive mirror of reality. Journalists should actively find ways to publicize a good cause, *even when there is no news value to it!* Likewise, undesirable causes should actively be denied exposure, even when there is real news value.

Of course "good" causes are Liberal ones. A close look at the social conscience of a journalist reveals the Liberal vision of the good society. "Social conscience" becomes just another word for the Liberal ideology described in an earlier chapter. Thus, social responsibility journalism becomes a rationalization for partisan activity on behalf of the Democratic political party and Liberal causes. That's why journalism is seen by many as a Liberal calling. Indeed many journalists readily admit that they became journalists "to do good," "to make a difference" and "to effect change." And of course that change is in the Liberal direction.

Muckraking is not a thing of the past. It is alive and well in today's newsrooms. Consider the following 30-second CNN promotion for its version of the news magazine, *Impact*. "The issues that define our times, the people who touch our lives, the questions that go unanswered, the problems that won't go away, if you think that nothing can be changed, see for yourself what can be done. Investigating, exposing, revealing stories that must be told. From CNN and *Time* comes the evolution of the news magazine, *Impact*, Sunday nine eastern on CNN."

Sounds very civic-minded. But journalists are only interested in raking the muck in the Republican camp. Journalists are very alert for Republican transgressions. As already noted, a pugnacious "us versus them" attitude dominates the coverage of leading Republicans, Conservative causes and institutions like the military. Thus, journalists use their "social responsibility" to rationalize partisan efforts make leading Republicans and Conservative causes unpopular.[3]

THE ELITE PRESS as POLITICAL INTEREST GROUP

In a democracy, **anyone trying to influence opinion is a politician.** While the press establishment does not act as a formal political party, with a formal structure and membership lists, it is an active and influential player in political campaigns. Members of the press seek to influence public policy and private behavior. They find ways to, in essence, endorse political candidates. They help Liberal activists get their message into the mass media. This is all done in the name of a higher good, of course. Be that as it may, this is not the activity of a non-partisan neutral press. It is the activity of a political interest group.

However, the press establishment is not just any old interest group. The evening news is the medium which all political players must employ to get their partisan messages out to the public. And during intense political combat over public opinion, the press establishment can't resist joining in the fray on the side of the Democratic party and Liberal causes. So, elite journalists are not honest brokers of information for a pluralistic news consuming public. They play favorites.

POLITICAL ADVERTISING

In the battle for public opinion, competing political interests work to get their partisan messages into the mass media. The outline of the conflict can be seen on contentious talk news programs like CNN's "CrossFire" and NBC's "The McLaughlin Group." The combatants do more than debate ideas about politics. Aware that millions of people are watching, these political combatants try to get their own partisan message out to the public while preventing their opponents from doing the same.

One technique to accomplish this is called "stepping on somebody's line" and it works like this.[4] When making a point, people often work up to it in a sequence of statements, with the last statement designed to stick in the viewer's mind. An opponent sees this coming and interrupts just as the speaker is about to deliver his key partisan message, thus preventing the audience from hearing something that might influence their thinking.

There are two kinds of advertisements, paid and unpaid. First are the paid political ads like the ones we see during election campaigns urging people to vote for some candidate. During every election, television carries a plethora of paid political ads touting this or that candidate, this or that cause. In a thirty- to-ninety-second ad, a politician gets out his partisan messages for a very hefty price. Wealthy candidates like H. Ross Perot can finance half hour advertisements on television called infomercials. Political players can buy television time or space in newspapers in order to publicize their cause or ideas. Paid advertising is very expensive.

However, the news itself provides another, less expensive way to get partisan messages to a mass audience. If a politician can do something journalists consider newsworthy, he (or she) can get into the news. When a journalist interviews a politician and that interview makes the evening news, the partisan political message is embedded in the news *for free*. That's the game. Competing partisans try to get their political messages into the news as they battle for public opinion. Since expensive air time was not purchased, it is called, "free advertising." Viewers who doesn't recognize this as advertising are less skeptical

The elite press makes it obscenely easy for Democrats to get free advertising. Democrats habitually get free advertising from the entire mass communication media --- from the movies to television dramas, situation comedies and PBS documentaries as well as the mainstream press.

However, Republicans are treated less generously. Liberal journalists interfere with Republican attempts to free advertising. Yes, they get their messages into the news, but the press distorts those messages. I call this "free but contested advertising." Even when Republicans pay television networks to air political commercials, their advertising does not go unchallenged. For instance, a television journalist may do a so-called "reality check." He will go through a Republican political ad, point by point, telling news consumers what he thinks is true or false. However, there is good reason to believe that the political prejudices of elite journalists distort the "reality checks" they perform.

When Republicans successfully beat up the image of a leading Democrat, the press will intervene on behalf of the Democrats. However, when Democrats are scoring political points against Republicans, the same Liberal press is very slow to deploy their truth squad. Even if the Democrats are promoting obvious fictions, the press will do little to set the record straight, as long as the Democrats are generating public relations capital.[5] The press jealously guards the good image of leading Democrats, rarely doing tough and timely "reality checks" on them.[6]

Interviews may give Republicans the opportunity slip in a little unpaid political advertising. However, Republican are forced to include the Democratic attack message, via the interviewing journalist, in their unpaid advertising. It works like this. Think of an interview as a sequence of messages. Some of the messages are comments from the Republican. Other messages are questions from the journalist. Some of those questions are attack questions crafted from the point of view of a partisan Democrat. These questions are not questions at all. They are mini-attack-ads automatically included in the interview.

Attacking opponents is standard operating procedure for all people engaged in politics, including journalists. That's because attack advertising works. Well-crafted political attacks can seriously damage the popularity of a public official. Negative public opinion of a public official can weaken or limit his capacity to do his job. If the negatives are high enough, an official might even be removed from office. It's a vicious game.

At least one journalist thinks that press attacks can influence public opinion, as this telling quote from correspondent Eleanor Clift of *Newsweek* during the 1992 presidential campaign indicates, "The press is beginning to draw some blood from the [H. Ross] Perot balloon and I think that will catch up with the [public opinion] numbers, eventually!"[7] Remember that the 1992 presidential election was a three-way race between Democrat William Clinton, Republican George Bush and Reform Party candidate H. Ross Perot. Perot was very popular when he first entered the 1992 presidential campaign and for a while it seemed possible for him to actually win.

THE POWER OF THE PRESS

But the public opinion game is more than getting people to change their minds. It's about getting people to do something. When politicians try to influence public opinion, they are ultimately trying to motivate people to vote for a certain candidate or lobby for a certain policy. Putting some of the above ideas together suggests that, *the power of press is its ability to use news images to motivate a certain percentage of the population to take some sort of action.* The Watergate Scandal provides a good example.

In 1973-74, the Nixon-hating press intended that news consumers have a bad image of President Nixon.[8] But, despite much reporting on the Watergate Scandal, public opinion was still on the side of the President. News consumers had a different image of the Watergate events than the Liberal press. The press had inadvertently put the Watergate into the "politics as usual" framework. Thus, people just shrugged their collective shoulders. The Watergate story went on in this fashion for some time. Public opinion changed, however, when journalists began covering the story as serious wrongdoing well beyond ordinary politics. The press created the image of President Nixon as an unrepentant criminal. It was that image of criminal wrongdoing that moved public opinion against President Nixon. Politicians responded to that change in opinion and began to take action against President Nixon. And that is what brought President Nixon down. It is important to note that there never was a so-called "smoking gun," proving beyond reasonable doubt that President Nixon was guilty of any crime.

Abusing their position as democracy's information brokers, journalists are active players in the public opinion game. But are Democrats and journalists engaged in a premeditated sinister plot? Probably not. Likely they do not meet in the basement of the *New York Times* to plot how they are going to stick it to the Republicans. They do not have to do that. It could be done with winks and nods. This is how things are rigged in other sectors of society. For instance, corporations can illegally fix prices of a product, without the advantage of covert face-to-face meetings. Journalists are so like-minded, they can easily fix news images with only their political instinct as a guide.

While they are not information dictators, the press can focus public attention the alleged improprieties of almost anyone they do not like, usually a Republican. And the press can limit the public relations damage to anyone they like, usually a Democrat. However, such meddling in the democratic process is not always as successful as it was during Watergate. Influencing public opinion is more art than predictable science. Journalists are not always able to slip the right messages into the news. Sometimes Republicans get their motivational messages into the news unscathed. When that happens, journalists are furious. The point is that just because the Liberal press does not always win the public opinion game, does not mean that they don't always try for the winning impression.

THE WINNING IMPRESSION

All successful advertising creates a winning impression. Employing the art of suggestion, commercial advertisers try to create the impression that if you buy their product you will become happier, healthier, sexier or richer.

Political ads are not a lot different. Political ads also employ the art of suggestion. These ads lead people to believe that their lives will be better if they would only vote for the right candidate or support the right public policy. At the heart of any winning media campaign is a winning impression.

Journalists are not content to merely report on this battle for public opinion. They can't resist joining the battle, helping friends and hurting enemies. The Liberal press uses the very same weapon, the art of suggestion. To the extent there is a Conservative press, they do the same. To get an idea on how they do it, let's examine how the news is created.

To start with, journalists are fundamentally storytellers. When describing an event, a storyteller does not tell all. That would leave the audience confused and bored. A storyteller must select part of an event and weave a narrative story around it. What the storyteller chooses to tell and how he chooses to tells it automatically incorporates non-verbal messages into the fabric of his story. If a storyteller does a good job, the audience will experience some sense of reality, even when the story is pure fiction.

Television journalists utilize the same production techniques as movie-makers. Like movie-makers, they integrate narration, photographs, computer graphics, video and commentary into a sequence of images which imitates real events. That sequence of media images is called "television news."

Like movie-makers, television journalists try to persuade news consumers to suspend disbelief and accept their constructed image as real. Like movie-makers, they try to get their audience to forget that the news is told from a definite point of view. When successful, journalists create the illusion that viewers are watching world events as they actually happen. The capacity to create an illusion of reality is the source of press credibility. That is, the news is credible to the extent it seems real to news consumers.

Consider the reporting of a simple political event as diagramed above. An event occurs. A journalist observes it. He then writes a news story which is illustrated by some video of the actual event. The movie-like product, the news image, is then aired on the evening news. News consumers watch the evening news, which creates an illusion of the event in their minds. Individual news consumers make their own interpretation of the news image. Different people will form different mental images of the same event. Finally, people called pollsters take a statistically designed sample of those individual opinions and produce something called *public opinion*.

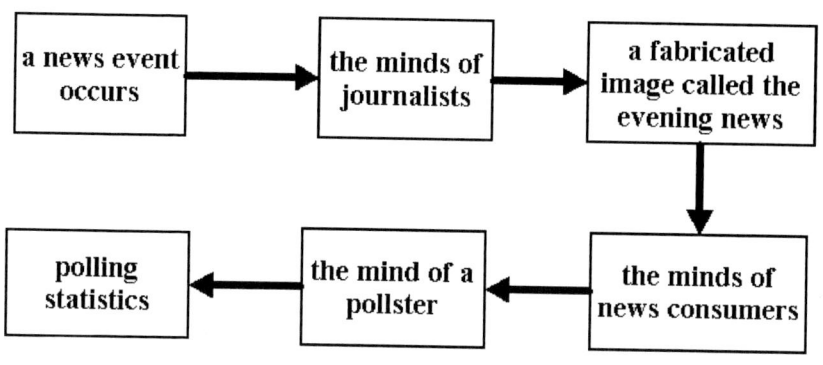

THE INFORMATION STREAM

During intense partisan battles for public opinion, many journalists let their partisan passions guide the production of news. This is a key idea. **The very production of the news automatically incorporates a context of implications, hints and cues into the context of the news.** Those contextual suggestions are what I call, **spin**. (The next chapter contains an extended discussion of spin.) When journalists manipulate these hints and cues to achieve partisan goals, contextual spin becomes political advertising.

Viewers easily detect and respond to those little contextual messages. Paying attention to unspoken contextual messages is a basic linguistic skill. We all learn to glean important information from the unguarded words of others. The common expression, "reading between the lines," attests to the sensitivity of people to contextual speech. Research confirms the idea that people are very sensitive to contextual communication. Studies show that small differences in the wording of questions asked by takers of opinion polls cause large change in the *measurement* of public opinion.[9] "Converging evidence from several behavioral sciences indicates that people are exquisitely sensitive to contextual cues when they make decisions, formulate judgements, or express opinions."[10]

There is good reason to believe that small changes in the contextual messages of the evening news can influence public opinion. "If language variations are capable of influencing opinion responses so powerfully, however, it seems likely that alternate forms of television news presentations should also evoke similar variability in political choices and preference." Evidently people are very sensitive to small changes in the information stream that reaches them from the mass media.

Thus, **journalists can influence public opinion by planting little hints, cues and suggestions into the news.** Spin is the sum total of those suggestions intended to influence public opinion. Journalists will occasionally reinforce their implicit messages with an explicit statement like an actor doing an aside to the audience, making sure it understands the message. But for the most part, press spin is the covert voice of journalists speaking from "between the lines" of the news trying to employ that winning impression.

Politicians understand that it takes only a few words and pictures to produce a compelling image that will make a winning impression. They pay millions of dollars for a 30-second message to be aired along with all the other advertising, news and entertainment on television. During the years of Republican Presidents, the 1970s and 1980s, journalists were outraged over the effectiveness of Republican political advertising and reported at length about it. They said, in essence, that Republican ads created false, but winning impressions. Listening to journalists, you would have gotten the idea that a false political message (the Willy Horton ad) handed out in 30-second chunks during the 1988 presidential campaign single-handedly defeated the Democratic candidate for President. This is passive acknowledgment that a very small amount of bias, in the form of political ads, can substantially alter public opinion.[11]

If a 30-second paid political ad can influence public opinion, then 30 seconds of political bias on the evening news should also influence public opinion. In fact, thirty seconds of biased news ought to be even more effective. Surely truth-telling journalists have more credibility with the public than any paid political ad. It is important to observe that a small change in the contextual shape of the evening news can cause large changes in the *news image* of an event which, in turn, changes the impression in the minds of a significant portion of the public.

Winning a political contest is usually about leading voters to believe something of a partisan nature. While Liberal journalists hotly deny that they are engaged in any partisan activity, they do understand how ostensively neutral information can be used to achieve partisan goals. Or at least they understand how Republicans can use unbiased information in the pursuit of partisan goals. Consider a comment from Ms. Elizabeth Arnold of National Public Radio (NPR).

First some background. In the winter of 1996-97 the Republican Speaker of the House of Representatives, Newt Gingrich, was accused by Democrats of various ethics transgressions. One accusation was that a college course, *Renewing America*, taught by Gingrich while he was Speaker, was partisan in nature and therefore violated House ethics rules. (Speaker Gingrich is a former college professor.)

Every Friday a group of elite journalists gather at PBS to discuss the previous week's events. The news talk show is called *Washington Week in Review*. The alleged ethics violations of Speaker Gingrich were discussed on the January 17, 1997, airing. The journalists were discussing the ethics of teaching a college course while a member of Congress. Referring to a recent speech delivered by Speaker Gingrich at the Republican National Committee winter meeting, Arnold said that Gingrich, "launched into what is at the center of this controversy, in a way, and that is, his classic speech, that we've all heard before, of renewing American civilization. Went right back into it. ... His speech, it's, it's, it's demonstrative because, the speech, it's all over the map. It's about replacing the welfare state. It's about scientific advancement. It's about cutting out food coupons. It's all over. In a way anyone could give this speech. In a way it's not partisan. And that's what his lawyers were saying today. But, *the goal of that speech is partisan*." [emphasis added] Clearly Arnold understands how non-partisan information can be used to achieve partisan goals.

College courses and the evening news are very much alike. Both are organized presentations of information which tell a story that is presumably true. If a college course can have a partisan goal, so can the evening news. Surely journalists understand this. Critics of the Liberal press certainly understand that, **journalists need not disseminate obviously biased news products to be guilty of using the news to achieve partisan goals.**

KEY IDEA

Media bias should be understood in terms of public opinion. The actual amount of bias is not important. That's because, it does not take much bias to influence public opinion.

SUMMARY

The Liberal press facilitates the public relations operations of leading Democrats, especially during political disputes. The Democrats provide the pictures and sound bites required for the Liberal press to help Democrats get their message into the news free of charge. It is a charade at the expense of the truth. It is a matter of selecting the truth for partisan gain.

Since television is the primary source of news for the vast majority of citizens, TV journalists have great power to influence public opinion. Television news shapes the image of current events in the minds of a significant percentage of the news consuming public. Television news employs the same techniques as commercial advertisers. Commercial ads rely on questionable impressions. Television pitchmen urge viewers to believe that they will become sexier, richer, healthier or happier if they buy this or that product. Television journalists urge people to believe that they will have a better life if they buy into the name brand ideas of the Democrats and not go for the Brand X policies of the Republicans.

Television journalists cut off fragments of reality and paste them together into an image of current events. Like a well-crafted movie, the evening news can be compelling, making it difficult for the audience to perceive the cut and paste job. Like movie-makers journalists create the illusion that something real is unfolding before the eyes of the viewers.

Real or contrived, news images projected to mass audiences influence public opinion statistics. All partisans, presidents, senators, governors and political activists understand this. They have no choice but to deal with the press, if they hope to stay in the public opinion business. They all know that news stories affect the image that many individual voters form of politicians.[12]

And most importantly, it does not take much tinkering with the news to have a powerful effect on public opinion. It takes only a few contextual cues and hints to influence opinion. Thus, the press can influence public opinion by manipulating the contextual messages in the news. The sum of those contextual messages is spin, which will be discussed in the next chapter.

DISCUSSION

When I first examined press favoritism, I concluded that it was largely the result of unconscious cognitive prejudices favoring the Democratic party and Liberal ideas. But when I studied the press coverage of political scandals, I became aware of the public opinion component. I then noticed that Democrats involved in a scandal seemed to get a lot of free, unopposed airtime to counter Republican scandalmongers. (The press was not so gracious to Republicans.) Further study suggested that favoritism in the press seems to be correlated with the public opinion efforts of the Democrats. I concluded that the touchstone for media bias is the partisan battle for public opinion.

Thus, a discussion of media bias is largely a discussion of political advertising and how it gets into the news. To say that a politician is sold as one would sell soap is to say nothing except that said politician is engaged in the political process. All winning politicians advertise. All winning politicians employ the techniques of salesmanship. As far as the news consumer is concerned, a message is a message, whether paid or unpaid.

Journalists sometimes talk about something called *public image*. For example, "The public image of the Republican party is uncaring and mean." But there is no such thing. No one image of anybody will fit the millions of individual images in the heads of citizens. We live a large diverse society, so there are many images in any comprehensive polling data. Some voters indeed have an image of Republicans as uncaring and mean. They are called Democrats. Some voters have a very positive image of Republicans. They are called Republicans. And millions more have all manner of images of Republicans. Thus, the public image of Republicans (or anyone else) does not actually exist. *There is no such thing as a single public image of anything!* Only complex statistics of public opinion supporting *multiple images* exist in the real world.

EXAMPLE: A Nice Conservative

When the Republican candidate for president, Robert Dole, chose Mr. Jack Kemp as his running mate in the 1996 election, journalist Schneider of CNN responded on August 9th with the usual political stereotyping. "He [Jack Kemp] is that rare combination, *a nice Conservative.* The face of Conservatism these days is too often mean or grouchy or intolerant." This prejudiced statement tells news consumers more about Mr. Schneider and CNN than about Conservatives. "The face of Conservatism" is just another way of saying, the *public image* of Conservatism.

But single public images do not exist. To be sure some people have this ugly image of Conservatism. They are called political Liberals. Other segments of society have different images of Conservatism. Many Libertarians and Populists share Conservative ideas. Conservatism itself has multiple images. When Schneider talks about the ugly face of Conservatism, he is selecting the part of public opinion which fits his stereotype of Republicans. Since public images like "the face of Conservatism" do not actually exist, Schneider is likely talking about *the news image* constructed by journalists and/or the image in his own head. Thus, the idea of a public image is just a rhetorical device which allows journalists to present stereotypes as proven fact.

END NOTES

(1)   See pages vi and 29 of **The Muckrakers and American Society**, Edited by Herbert Shapiro, D.C. Heath and Company, Boston, 1968.

(2)   See pages 24-25 of **Mass Media and American Politics** (third edition), by Doris A. Graber, CQ Press, Washington, D.C., 1989, for a discussion of social responsibility journalism. For a more complete discussion, see chapter three of *Four Theories of the Press*, by Fred Siebert, Theodore Peterson and Wilbur Schramm, University of Illinois Press, Chicago, 1963. In my opinion, the practice of using the news as free advertisement for favored political causes is an abuse of press power.

(3) To rationalize is "to attribute (one's actions) to rational and creditable motives without analysis of true and especially unconscious motives" or "to provide plausible but untrue reasons for conduct." (*Webster's Ninth New Collegiate Dictionary*).

(4) The expression comes from drama. When one actor is delivering his lines and another actor begins speaking before the script calls for it, the second actor is said to "step on the line."

(5) A good example of the watchdog that failed to bark is the coverage of budget battles between a Republican Congress and a Democratic President. This was especially evident when Democrats accused the Republicans of cutting the Federal Medicare Program, when they actually planned to increase the per capita spending from $4,500 to $7,200. It was an excellent example of the big lie and the press did nothing. For more on this subject, see the example in the next chapter.

(6) This disparity in the coverage of political groups can be explained by the social psychology of political groups. Liberals in the press are ideologically provincial. Their political prejudices tell them that they know the truth and Conservatives don't. In other words, God is a Liberal. Conservatives' beliefs are outside the realm of acceptable opinion. Thus, there is no imperative to give Conservatives equal time. In fact, the press seems to feel that it must protect the public from dangerous Conservative ideas by putting them ideas into "context."

(7) This comment was made by Ms. Clift on NBC's *MacLaughlin Group* during a discussion of the 1992 presidential campaign. At the time she was a senior correspondent. As of this writing she is a senior editor of *Newsweek*.

(8) I don't use the word "hate" casually. Nixon-hating has been a badge of righteous accomplishment worn by many journalists. Consider this statement from journalist Eileen Shanahan," I hated Richard Nixon with a passion, I don't mind saying." At a journalism seminar, she was making the point that as a professional journalist she was able overcome her strong feelings and still be fair to Richard Nixon. She made this comment at a meeting at the School

of Communication, at American University, which was aired on C-SPAN, February 2, 1989.

(9) For an overview of the question-wording literature, see Schuman, David and Stanley Presser, 1982, **Questions and Answers in Attitude Surveys**: Experiments on question form, wording and context published by Academic Press in New York. Also see McClendon, McKee and David O'Brien, Question-order effects on subjective well-being, volume 52 of *Public Opinion Quarterly*, pages 351-364. "Although most of the research into framing of political opinions rests on survey evidence, there is a growing experimental literature concerning the effects of perceiving stimuli as either gains or losses on political judgements." published in 1988. And see Quattrone, George and Amos Tversky, Contrasting Rational and Psychological Analysis of Political Choice, a paper published in *American Political Science Review* in 1988. And see Ansolabehere, Stephen, Shanto Iyengar, and Aam Simon, Good news, Bad News, and Economic Voting, a paper presented at the Annual Meeting of the American Political Science Association in 1990

(10) This quote introduces chapter 2 of **Is Anyone Responsible** by Shanto Iyengar, published by The University of Chicago Press, Chicago, 1991.

(11) The Liberal press saw Republican ads as a major threat to democracy. They exerted significant energy to counter them. The ad watches of 1988 and 1992 are examples. Since the election of Liberal Democrat William Clinton, the interest in Republican ads has subsided for some reason.

(12) There is plenty of evidence supporting the idea that the news affects public opinion. See page 217 of **Good Intentions Make Bad News** by S. Robert Lichter and Richard Noyes of the Center for Media and Public Affairs, published by Rowan & Littlefield Publishers, Inc., Lanham, Maryland, in 1995. Also see page 125 of **Out of Order** by Thomas E. Patterson, published by Alfred A. Knopf, in New York, in 1993.

Chapter 7

PARTISAN SPIN

It was called the "splendid deception." During the 1930s and 1940s, Democratic President Franklin Roosevelt conspired with the press to deceive the American people about the state of his health. It turns out that President Roosevelt could not "walk or stand without help."[1] He was stricken by polio in 1921, leaving him paralyzed from the waist down. He wore braces on his legs and could stand only for short periods time, and he needed help to do that. The press hid that fact from the public.

Journalists did not take pictures of Roosevelt in a wheelchair. Out of thousands of pictures in the Roosevelt library, only two of Roosevelt in a wheelchair exist. A self imposed *code of silence* prevented journalists from taking any picture that would reveal his condition. "If a new reporter or a new photographer came on the scene and tried to snap a picture of Roosevelt in his wheelchair, looking crippled being carried, the older photographer would knock the camera to ground or block the shot with his body."[2] No newsreels show him in a wheelchair.

Political cartoonists were in on the deception. No cartoons showed Roosevelt's condition. Quite the opposite. Cartoons showed a physically active president. The conspiracy was stunningly successful.

Why were journalists so willing to help the Democrats deceive the public? Journalists and academic apologists like Doris Karns Goodwin claim, "it was the only decent thing to do." However, I think that the motivation was somewhat less praiseworthy. According to one journalist from the era, "ninety seven percent of the press was heart and soul with Roosevelt."[3] Like today's journalists, the press corps of the 1930s favored the Democratic party and Liberal (progressive) policies.

And there was good reason to believe that Roosevelt could not attain high office if voters knew he was a paraplegic. "In the 1920s, to be handicapped in some visible way carried with it social opprobrium."[4] I think it reasonable to assume that attitude persisted in 1932, when Roosevelt ran for president. It makes sense to conclude that the many people would not have voted for a cripple. I think it is reasonable to assume that journalists understood this. And since journalists favored the Democratic party and its Liberal policies, a Republican win would have been a defeat for the press. Thus it follows that the elite press deceived the voters in pursuit of their own partisan goals.

The *splendid deception* did not require heavy-handed propaganda to fool the public. It is well known that such techniques of persuasion do not work very well.[5] The willing accomplices of the Liberal press performed their task indirectly. Journalists did not actually say Roosevelt could walk. They led people to believe that Roosevelt could walk! A partisan press gave the fictional **impression** that Roosevelt could actually walk.

FICTIONAL IMPRESSIONS

Misleading fictional impressions are the weapon of choice in the battle for public opinion. Republicans, Democrats, Conservatives and Liberals all promote self-serving fictions in hopes of gaining popularity for themselves and unpopularity for their opponents.[6] Journalists also play the game. They can't seem to resist imparting a partisan spin as information moves from the scene of a news event to the news consumer.

Key to understanding spin is to note that the very production of the news automatically incorporates a context of implications, hints and cues into the context of the news. If there were no bias in the news, those contextual suggestions would be random. But of course they are not. Most of the time, spin favors the Democratic party and Liberal causes.

In a very real way, spin is the covert voice of journalists speaking to news consumers from "between the lines" trying to influence public opinion. Like all other political players, the Liberal press seeks to discover and employ winning impressions. A favored way to construct a fictional impression is to simply leave out an important part of the story, as the following example illustrates.

EXAMPLE: A Fictional Air Fare

In the spring of 1991 the press reported that the chief of staff to Republican President George Bush, Mr. John Sununu, was taking an excessive number of plane trips, leaving the taxpayers with the bill. Journalists claimed that Sununu stuck it to the taxpayers to the tune of $12,000 per hour of flight time. For instance journalist Randall Pinkston of CBS reported on April 21, 1991 that Sununu had left the taxpayers with a bill of $30,000 for a single trip to Colorado. He suggested that Sununu had gotten away with paying only $1,100. The clear implication was that the taxpayers would not have gotten billed for the $30,000 if Sununu had not taken the trip to Colorado.

Suspicious of that implication, I called the Defense Department to see if I could uncover the facts Pinkston did not present.

It turned out that the press had seriously misrepresented the truth. When the government says that it costs X dollars to take a trip, they don't calculate the cost the same way we might calculate the cost of a family trip. When the government says a trip cost X dollars, they include much more than the incidental "out-of-pocket" expenses. They include the *total* cost of having the aircraft in the hanger *ready to fly*. When ordinary people consider the cost of a trip, they do not usually consider the cost to have the family car in the garage ready to go!

To illustrate the difference, suppose you plan a trip to Colorado and want to compute the cost. You will add the cost of gas, food, lodging, entertainment and other miscellaneous costs. When you say that a trip cost you $1,800, you are referring to those operational costs paid out of pocket. You don't figure the cost of purchasing the car and keeping it maintained and ready for the trip to Colorado. You probably didn't count these fixed costs when you said that the trip to Colorado would cost $1,800. But the government does exactly that. When the government tells you that a trip costs $12,000, they include the fixed and operational costs.

The government computes the costs of trips as operational plus the fixed costs. Fixed costs are those expenses which are necessary just to be in the business of flying government officials from one place to another. Fixed costs include cost of: (1) purchasing the aircraft, (2) maintenance and (3) the wages of pilot and air crew as well as the ground crew. In other words, the fixed cost is the cost to procure the airplane and keep it in the hanger with the crew standing by ready to fly. This is key. *Whether the plane flies or not, taxpayers pick up the fixed costs!* Operational costs are the costs incurred while operating a military aircraft. These include fuel, food, landing fees and pilot time above aircraft readiness and maintenance time.

So what was the fixed cost of Sununu's Boeing 707? My Defense Department sources told me that most of the $12,000 per flight hour is taken up by the fixed cost. I was told that the operational costs are typically very small, amounting to a few hundred dollars an hour.

What journalist Randall Pinkston of CBS said was technically true. That probably was his rationalization for telling the story the way he did. Yes, the taxpayers had to pick up a bill of some $30,000 for the trip to Colorado. But suppose Sununu did not fly to Colorado. What is the cost to the taxpayers in that case? The taxpayers would still pay nearly all of it! Since most of the $30,000 represents fixed costs, it would have been absorbed by all the other flights made during the year increasing the fixed cost per hour for those flights. So, Sununu did not stick the taxpayers with a $30,000 bill as reported by the press. The operational costs were probably around $1,000!

Why did CBS and other news organizations lead news consumers to believe that the out-of-pocket operational costs to the taxpayers for flying a Boeing 707 were $12,000 an hour? Did the highly educated and very talented journalists of the elite Washington press corps actually fail to get the story? It took me only a half an hour of phone calls to discover that Sununu's trip to Colorado was cost considerably less than $30,000. I find it difficult to believe that journalists failed to do the same.

I think that journalists were so intent on turning public opinion against a popular Republican president that they were motivated to mislead news consumers. Remember that it was just after the Gulf War. The press was resoundingly defeated in its attempts to make the war unpopular. The popularity rating of George Bush had reached over 90 percent. The Liberal Democrats that comprise 89 percent of the Washington press corps must have been eager to take a nip out of that popularity. And they were not going to let the facts get in their way.

While the promoters of political fictions often rely on the absence of salient information, they also use loaded words. Sometimes it may take only a single well-chosen word to construct a winning impression, causing large shifts in public opinion. In one interesting case it took only a single word. I'm referring to the press coverage of the partisan battle between Republicans and Democrats over the federal budget during the winter of 1995-96.

EXAMPLE: <u>Medicare "Cuts" versus "Savings"</u>

In the fall of 1995, Congressional Republicans proposed to increase spending on Medicare by some 7 percent. Democrats wanted to spend slightly more, about 7.9 percent. Democrats employed a partisan fiction in an effort to make Republicans unpopular. In a big lie campaign, Democrats accused the Republicans of slashing the federal Medicare program.

Rather than tell news consumers the truth, the elite press helped the Democrats spread the political fiction. Many journalists repeated the Medicare "cutting" canard as proven fact, reinforcing and validating the attack fiction. As the budget battle heated up, journalists seized many opportunities to imply indirectly that Republicans were *cutting* Medicare. And on occasion journalists fortified the fiction by openly declaring that Republicans were cutting Medicare.

On the 3rd of December 1995, ABC headlined its news story about the proposed Republican Medicare budget as the "UNKIND CUTS." Anchorperson Carol Simpson presented the following lead, "In Washington, what was supposed to be a productive week of budget negotiations turned into three days of finger pointing so acrimonious that talks broke down entirely. Both sides are still far apart with President Clinton still unwilling to make *the deep cuts* [emphasis added] in Medicare, education and the environment that the Congress wants. House Budget Committee Chairman John Kasich today defended Republican cuts in social services."

Then Simpson aired the following quote from Representative Kasich: "In each of the major entitlement programs, whether it's welfare, Medicare, Medicaid, each one of those programs are going to continue to go up and go up significantly. What we are trying to do is to stop them from going through the roof so they bring the whole country down."

Answering Congressman Kasich's comments, Simpson continued, "Republicans argue the *cutbacks* [emphasis added] in social programs can be made up by Americans offering more of their money and time to help the needy. But as ABC's Kevin Newman reports, that presents another problem." Mr. Newman went on to tell news consumers that it was proven fact that Republicans were wrong, wrong, wrong. By implication, the Democrats were right. He included a token comment from the Republican point of view in a misleading effort to project an image of fairness.

This report harmonized with the theme of the Democratic attack on Congressional Republicans. The Democratic party line at the time was that President Clinton was defending the aged, poor and sick against an extremist Republican Congress. Ms. Simpson echoed the party line when she said that "President Clinton is still unwilling to make the deep cuts in Medicare, education and the environment that the Congress wants." Repeating obvious political propaganda as proven fact exceeds all norms of fair and balanced journalism.

The Republicans were understandably outraged at this meddling in politics. There were many testy confrontations between Republicans and Liberal journalists over the usage of the word "cut." Some openly laughed at Republican efforts to get those journalists to tell the truth. While many journalists were incorrigible, others were less partisan. However, enough journalists insisted on using the word "cut" to describe the proposed 45 percent increase in Medicare to move public opinion.

With the help of their willing accomplices in the press, the Democrats were able to win a great public relations victory. Evidence appeared on the December 7, 1995, editorial page of the *Wall Street Journal*. They reported the shocking results of a public opinion poll. According to the poll, only 22 percent of the public knew that the Republicans wanted to increase the per person spending on Medicare from $4800 to $6700. Twenty-seven percent of the public thought that Republicans intended to cut per person Medicare spending below $4000! Twenty-four percent believed that Republicans would keep the per person spending at the current level. The remaining 25 percent did not have an opinion. *When told that Republicans were planning to increase Medicare spending by 45 percent, 60 percent of the people said that was too high!* This poll demonstrates that the press failed to properly inform the American electorate on an important political issue.

Journalists *remained mostly silent while Democrats lied to the voters.* Journalists strengthened the lie with the partisan use of labels in the news. When the Republicans proposed a 7 percent increase in Medicare, the press labeled it "a spending cut," hyping a harsh image of Medicare-slashing Republicans. During the intense budget debate many journalists clung to that loaded label, until the Democrats submitted their Medicare budget. When Democrats proposed a 7.9 percent increase in Medicare spending, the press turned on a linguistic dime and labeled that "a savings," transmitting an image of caring Democrats out to protect Medicare.[7]

Sometimes political fictions are overtly stated in narrative news stories. But more often, journalists speak to news consumers in the language of impressions. Using unspoken assumptions, suggestions, hints and cues imbedded in contextual environment of the days news, journalists communicate political fictions that sometimes influence public opinion. That is, journalists can manipulate public opinion merely by manipulating the contextual framework of the news.

And it's so easy. Partisan journalists can nourish the growth of those important political fictions merely by way they construct the evening news. As journalists construct news products, they have to make judgements and selections. One of those selections is which story is important and which is not. By simply promoting certain stories to the top of the news and other stories to the bottom of the news, a chain of contextual messages is automatically generated.

AGENDA SETTING

When journalists judge what story is important, they implant the first of a sequence of unspoken messages. These structural messages can have a powerful effect on public opinion. It works like this. People talk about what's in the news. Journalists put the news together; therefore they influence what people talk about. The power to influence what people talk about is called "the agenda-setting capacity of the press."[8]

What is an agenda? An agenda is a list of items to accomplish. When Republican Ronald Reagan became President in 1981, he had a political agenda that was: (1) increase military capability, (2) defeat Communism, and (3) reduce the size of the United States government. These were the three important goals he wanted to accomplish. Congressional Democrats wanted to accomplish just the opposite: (1) decrease our military capability, (2) reach an accommodation with Communism and (3) increase the size of the federal government. These differences formed the basis of the conflict between Liberals and Conservatives during the Cold War.

The elite press also has its list of things to accomplish. But journalists won't admit it. They play a kind of public opinion charade. For example, in late 1991 journalists told news consumers for weeks that health care was an important issue. Then they conducted an opinion poll to "discover" what people thought was important. And on the 28th of January, 1992, the anchor for ABC World News Tonight, Peter Jennings announced the "finding" that *the people* thought health care was important and wanted to hear what President George Bush was going to say about it in his State of the Union message to Congress. This is a charade because it was journalists who told people that health care was so important in the first place.

With little constraint from those who manage news organizations, the working press actively pursues its own political agenda. Like other political players, journalists internalize this partisan activity with a self-serving vision of doing good. However that is false on its face. By the time the elite press finishes telling us what is important, journalists have laid out the political agenda of the Liberal wing of the Democratic party!

I think a good working definition is as follows: *Agenda-setting is the ability of any person, group or compelling event to get people talking and thinking about some particular subject.* Left alone, people would focus their attention on what they consider the most vivid and compelling people and events. Different events would be vivid and compelling to different people, of course. This is especially true in our pluralistic democracy. In a perfect world, the news agenda would set itself and journalists would be the simple messengers who would present people the wide spectrum of information they want. The evening news would speak with many voices.

But the television press speaks with one voice and therefore becomes a key element in setting the public agenda. That's because most people get most of their news from television. People automatically take the top of the news to be important. Journalists understand this. Journalists know it is possible to influence public discussion merely by choosing what news stories to air. While claiming to be fair and balanced, elite journalists often promote to the top of the news stories that play to strengths of the Democratic party.

EXAMPLE: The 1984 Presidential Campaign

In that year, elite journalists pushed campaign issues that were to the disadvantage of the Republicans to the center of the news. A campaign issue is a point of public concern which a politician feels will yield favorable changes of public opinion. When Democrats made the age of Republican Ronald Reagan an issue, they were hoping that people would find President Reagan unacceptable and favor the Democrats. The press did its part. President Reagan's age was the second most covered issue that year. Of the top ten campaign issues covered by the press in 1984, only one cut against the Democrats.[9] The press stacked a news agenda with issues that were bad for Republicans.

The fact that the Democrats and the elite press lost the 1984 election does not mean that journalists did not set a biased agenda. Without an issues agenda that favored the Democrats, it is possible that the Republican victory may have been even larger.

Undeterred by their own favoritism, elite journalists assert that it is their democratic duty to set the agenda during election campaigns. Journalists think that they know the logically correct issues for any election. If the press agenda happens to help the Democrats, it only means that the Democrats are also logically correct.

Consider the so-called flag issue of the 1988 presidential election. Remember that the Cold War was still being fought at that time. Republicans wanted to defeat Communism. For them the flag symbolized the struggle of freedom against the tyranny of Communism. To Liberal Democrats the American flag symbolized American xenophobia. Journalists had a similar view. Many Liberal-minded journalists likewise did not perceive serious danger from Communism and, therefore, viewed the Cold War as a useless effort at best. For those journalists there was not much of an issue here.

Thus, the Republican campaign had to work very hard to get the flag issue on the public agenda. In an effort to influence the campaign agenda, Republican candidate George Bush made several so-called "photo op" visits to flag factories during the 1988 presidential campaign. Since many Liberal journalists perceived no need to fight the Cold War, this move was seen by many as a cynical appeal to patriotism for selfish political gain. Many journalists perceived Republican George Bush as a demagogue and openly ridiculed the flag factory trips. Much to the political chagrin of the elite press, Bush won this particular battle for the public agenda.

The importance assigned to an issue is not simply a matter of the number of times a story is carried. The placement of an issue in the news product also contributes to the importance of that issue. Where a story appears on the evening news signals to news consumers the importance of that news story. The evening television news has a format. First are the headlines at the start of the show. The first segment presents the most important news stories, usually about three. After a commercial break comes the news of secondary importance. Of course stories not shown at all are certainly not important. At about fifteen to twenty minutes into the network evening news are all the "back paged" stories of lesser importance. This is followed by a longer than usual story which is designed to focus and mold public opinion.

The way the news is defined sets the agenda and communicates to news consumers what is important and what is not. Typically, *journalists define the news in a way that favors the Democratic political party and Liberal ideas at the expense of the Republican party and Conservative ideas.* Small changes in the way journalists define news can have a powerful affect on what viewers consider important.

PRIMING PUBLIC OPINION

Agenda-setting has an interesting effect; it helps to prime the thinking of news consumers.[10] "By calling attention to some matters while ignoring others, television news influences the standards by which governments, presidents, policies, and candidates for public office are judged [by the public]."[11] By putting some information at the center of the news while pushing other information to the margins, journalist influence the standards people use to judge public figures. This is important because *a change in the standards by which people judge a politician will change public opinion of that politician.*

Cognitive psychology suggests an explanation of the *priming effect.* People tend not to make judgements after long and careful review of the data, information and relevant academic studies. That's because our mental capacities are limited while information is massive, complex, contradictory, confusing and incomplete. Typically we do not have time to evaluate all of it. And to complicate matters further, the exact piece of desired data is often not available. In order to get anything done, we do the intelligent thing: we take short cuts. That means that we rely on our beliefs and prejudices.

One way to tame the information tide is to simply not pay attention to all of it. And one way to do that is to trust that the right information will automatically come to mind when needed. This might be called the inspiration short cut and often works very well. Inspiration is something that just pops into our heads. Our recent experience tends to prime what pops into our heads. We then make evaluations based on what just popped into our heads. Thus, our recent experience tends to prime our evaluations of people and events.

The public opinion results from priming news consumers is predictable. That's because priming is the capacity of the news to change *"the standards people use to make political evaluations."*[12] My own examination of priming studies suggests that the press tries to prime our thinking in ways that favor the Democratic party and Liberal ideas.[13] In short, journalists try to get people to evaluate Democrats on their strengths and Republicans on their vulnerabilities. Of course, this is what competing partisans always try to do.

For example, during the 1988 campaign, the press thought the Republican candidate for Vice President, Dan Quayle, was vulnerable on what they saw as his lack of experience. More than one journalist stated that Quayle did not have the intelligence or stature to be "a heartbeat away from the presidency." The press told us that character was an important yardstick for measuring candidates for high public office. By airing a lot of stories on Quayle's perceived character flaws and ignoring his accomplishments, the press attempted to prime voters to judge him on that basis. The press even went back to his college days and tried to make him look like a draft dodger and a possible womanizer. There was no statute of limitations on this aggressively partisan reporting. But in the end, the press found no disqualifying character flaws they could substantiate.

The excuse given for the *close scrutiny* of Quayle was that he was not known to the American people. However, the 1992 Democratic candidate for President in 1992 was also not well-known. And there were real character issues associated with then Governor William Clinton; issues of dodging the draft, womanizing and a creative relationship with the truth surfaced during the primary campaign. But the press priming flip-flopped suggesting to voters that character should not be used as a standard to judge a candidate for President. In 1988 character was the deciding issue journalists used for judging a Vice President. In 1992, the press did its best to de-prime the character issue as a standard for judgement.

This partisan double standard for judging political figures persists to this writing. When evaluating Republican Vice President Quayle, every aspect of his character and every aspect of the job is fair game for close press scrutiny. However, Democrats get no such treatment. Yes, the press will tell us about the scandals surrounding President Clinton. However the priming will tell us that those scandals are not important. Taking the news stories and the priming together, we are told, in essence, that Democrat Clinton is a beloved rascal. We should still like him. If his cabinet members become involved in scandal, then Clinton should not be blamed. However, when Republican Presidents Reagan and Bush had scandal trouble with their aides, journalists quickly and eagerly blamed those Republican Presidents for the alleged wrongdoing of anyone who worked for them.

THE BLAME GAME

Blaming is characteristic of the prejudiced style of thinking. Partisans reflexively blame enemy out-groups for the bad things that happen. So does the elite press. Regardless of the situation or the actual facts, the Liberal press finds a way to blame Republicans. Political fiction often plays a key role in the blame game.

Consider the partisan debate over the increase of the national debt in the 1980s. Democrats and Republicans blamed each other for the size of the national debt. The presidency was controlled by the Republicans and the House of Representatives was controlled by the Democrats. According to the United States Constitution, all appropriations bills must originate in the House of Representatives. But for any bill to become law, that bill must also be signed by the President. The Democratic House of Representative and the Republican President had to agree for any budget bill to become law. Thus both were to blame.

Ignoring their own role in building the debt, the Democrats referred to the federal red ink as "the Reagan-Bush debt." Siding with the Democrats, the press also blamed the Republicans for the national debt. Consider some blame messages from *Wall Street Journal*. In a front page story of February 8, 1994, reporters David Wessel and David Rogers said, "Call it Ronald Reagan's revenge. The whopping deficit he left behind, together with the Bush-era caps on federal spending, has forced Bill Clinton to adopt many of his predecessors' spending cuts to pay for watered-down Democratic spending increases." Or look at this spin from CBS Washington Bureau Chief Barbara Cochran aired on C-SPAN's "Journalists Round Table" on September 23, 1994: "There's no question it was the Reagan tax cuts that led to the deficit." The partisan cognition was simple. Something bad (the national debt) happened and the Republicans were to blame.

Again in 1996, the press blamed Republicans. During a caustic partisan brawl over the 1996 federal budget, the Democratic President and the Republican Congress failed to reach agreement in time to pay many government workers. There was a partial shutdown of the federal government. The House of Representatives had passed a budget bill which the President subsequently vetoed. Even though the President had an equal hand in shutting down the government, the Democrats still blamed the Republicans. And the Democrats' willing accomplices in the press transformed this demagogic fiction into proven fact.

Besides the unearned sense of superiority, political blaming can accrue public relations rewards. That is, blame messages can influence public opinion. Blame is an often-used tool in the struggle for power in democracies. On many occasions, political factions have gained power by successfully blaming the opposition for some disaster. Seeming to understand this, the elite press blames Republicans, while protecting

Democrats from similar public relations damage. The elite press approves of Democrats and encourages news consumers to do the same.

APPROVAL AND DISAPPROVAL

Journalists persist in the practice of telling news consumers who rates public approval and who deserves disapproval. There is plenty of reason to believe that a Liberal press wants Democrats to win the battle for public opinion. Thus, journalists can't resist telling news consumers to approve of leading Democrats. Even when Democrats are using dishonest tactics in the battle for public opinion, the Liberal press rarely disapproves. Instead, they encourage us to admire the Democrats for their political ability.

EXAMPLE: Who Cares?

In January, 1996, President Clinton and the press staged a so-called news conference in which the president repeatedly referred to Republican Medicare cuts in the Republican budget. After the President's news conference, the Republican Speaker of the House of Representatives held his own news conference at which he criticized the President for "misrepresenting" Republican budget proposals. Using the partisan fiction that Republicans were cutting Medicare, the Democrats were getting good "traction" against the Republicans during the bitter partisan fighting over the United States budget. That Friday (January 12, 1996) PBS aired its news talk show, *Washington Week in Review.* The following conversation from that show is instructive.

Moderator Ken Bodie noted, "The Speaker said that the President was quote, 'factually challenged,' in that news conference. He [Speaker Newt Gingrich] said the news conference itself was destructive and that it was nothing but a political game."

Gloria Borger of *U.S. News and World Report*, said with a laugh, "Well, ... two out three ain't bad. Naah, I think, ... I think, You know Clinton held a press conference to try to calm the markets. And what he did was to set off Newt Gingrich like a rocket. You know Ken, he knew exactly what he was doing as Mara was saying, ... pulled his chain, talking about deep cuts in Medicare."

Pounding her fist on the table in mock anger, **Borger** continued, "And what Gingrich was so upset about was he said, 'he knows that what we're doing is we're, we're, we're ah, we've got a hundred and sixty-eight billion in *savings* in Medicare. [emphasis added] We're not making these deep cuts. He [Speaker Gingrich] practically called him [President Clinton] a liar. Clinton knew exactly what was going on here. And I think what we may be seeing here is the end game. These folks positioning themselves because the [budget] deal may ultimately break down. They don't want to have their fingerprints all over that. So, Clinton is sounding optimistic, 'Yes we are going to get a budget deal.' And Newt Gingrich is saying that, 'he [the President] is not playing fair and square.' And then who is the public to blame?"

Notice that Ms. Borger fails to address the question of the President's honesty. She is suggesting here that it's not important that President Clinton had lied to the public. Instead she implies that he *deserves* approval for his political acumen. The fact that these Medicare fictions made it difficult for citizens to make informed decisions were of no apparent concern to her. Notice also that Borger was concerned with the blame game, suggesting that people should blame Republicans.

However, when Republicans are kicking Democratic butt, the attitude of the press does a 180-degree turn. They do not encourage news consumers to admire the political acumen of Republicans. The response of the elite press to the 1988 presidential election is a good example. Many journalists believe that Democratic Governor Michael Dukakis lost the presidential election in 1988, in large part, because he did not effectively counter Republican attack ads that ran on television. According to this partisan mythology, popular in the press and Democratic circles, Republicans used deceptive television ads to kick Democrat Dukakis out of the running for President. Even though the 1988 Republican ad campaign was adroit and successful, the press encouraged news consumers to condemn Republicans.

VERBAL SPIN

When did you stop beating your wife?

Direct meaning	Implied Meaning
A simple request for information.	The person being questioned is a married man. He used to beat his wife and has stopped

Besides the powerful but subtle contextual cues implanted in the news by agenda-setting, priming and blaming, the elite press adds a verbal spin to the mix. Verbal spin employs the language of suggestion and insinuation. Suppose a journalist sticks a microphone in your face and asks, "When did you stop beating your wife?" This may appear to be a simple request for information. A reporter just doing his job. But the question carries unspoken baggage. It assumes that you are a male, that you are married, that you used to beat your wife and that you have stopped. But if you never beat your wife, the question becomes an unfounded accusation. If you are not married, the question becomes absurd. This question has come to symbolize the idea that questions have assumptions as the above diagram illustrates.

The statement has two meanings. First, there is the direct message, "When did you stop beating your wife?" Second, there are the three contextual assumptions shown above on the right. These assumptions give meaning to the stated question. Without that context, the question would have little meaning. The unspoken contextual assumptions are communicated right along with the question. Journalists often take advantage of this indirect characteristic of communication. Suppose Mr. Journalist is still convinced, after all your denials, that you beat your wife. But he does not have "the facts" to go with the story. Without violating any journalist ethics or norms, he can still find a way to suggest that you actually do beat your wife without directly saying so.

Journalists skillfully employ verbal spin. It is important to note that it does not take much to do the job -- a tweaked sentence, a loaded word, or other subtle changes in tone and texture. Journalists know how to use the techniques of indirect speech to paint an image of people and events which they can't justify with actual facts. Remember the fiction that "Republicans are cutting Medicare" discussed above. In that case, the press used the simple device of loaded words to carry its partisan message.

Loaded Words

During the 1995-96 Budget debate between the Democratic President and the Republican Congress, both Republicans and Democrats proposed slowing the growth in the Federal Medicare program. When talking about the Republican budget proposals, journalists often used the word "cut." The word "cut" in this context gives the impression that Republicans were proposing to spend less on Medicare. Journalists energetically argued on television that the word "cut" was the right word to describe what the Republicans wanted to do to Medicare. However, the same journalists were loath to use the word "cut" when talking about Democratic budget proposals. Instead they used the word "savings." The word "savings" has a good ring to it.

Using "savings" and "cuts" to refer to the same thing is a good example of loaded words. This tricky use of words is the sort of thing invented by public relations people, especially political consultants. Indeed, Democrats used this pair of loaded words to good effect. I doubt that the Democrats would have been so successful without an evening news which so effectively harmonized with the Democratic use of these loaded words,

The press engages in other word loading mischief. They tell us that "liberal" is good and "conservative" is bad. That is, journalists often associate the word "conservative" with things bad and the word "liberal" with things good.

Consider the coverage of foreign affairs. The press often dramatizes conflict in authoritarian countries using a morality play format. People supporting democratic institutions are referred to as "liberals" and characterized as heroes. People working on behalf of the more authoritarian forces are referred to as "conservatives," and are cast as the villains of the piece. Since the end of the Cold War, elite journalists often use this simplistic good versus evil paradigm in news reports on political struggles in formerly Communist countries.

When covering the abortion debate, journalists use politically loaded words to describe the issue. People (mostly Liberals) who favor the right of a woman to abortion call themselves "pro-choice." People who oppose Liberals are seen to be taking rights away from the mother. Liberals call them "anti-abortionists." People who oppose abortion call themselves "pro-life" because they think the fetus has a right to life. The press uses loaded labels by characterizing the issue as a dispute between "pro-choice" advocates and "anti-abortionists."

Journalists also use loaded labels in their coverage of the private ownership of firearms. Journalists use the loaded term "gun control." The phrase "gun control" frames the issue as one of "control" and not one of "rights." This is the Liberal point of view. Liberals believe that citizens do not have any constitutional right to own a firearm. By using the term "gun control" the press sides with the Liberal Democrats on the issue. Conservatives and Libertarians on the other hand see the issue as one of rights. They believe that citizens have a fundamental constitutional "right to keep and bear arms."

It should be noted that the Conservative press, to the extent it exists, loads words to favor the Republican party and Conservative ideas. Loaded words subtly suggest to news consumers that a particular point of view is the correct one. When journalists consistently employ politically loaded words, they reveal their intent to meddle with public opinion. The result is a false image of people and events.

Twisted Words

It is characteristic of the partisan style of verbal behavior to twist the words of opponents in an attempt to make them unpopular. Partisans frequently interpret statements made by political opponents in a way calculated to make them look bad. Word twisting conforms to the "us versus them" partisan attitude described in chapter three. Elite journalists are accomplished in the art of word twisting.

Suppose Mr. Republican candidate says that he will "do whatever it takes" to get elected, meaning that he will work very hard, press door bells, hug babies, and be interrogated by hostile journalists. He means that he will do whatever is legal, moral and ethical to accomplish the task of getting elected. However, Liberals in the press are likely to leave out the implied bit about "legal, moral and ethical," thus twisting the obvious meaning of the statement into an admission of something sinister.

EXAMPLE: <u>Twisting Speaker Gingrich</u>

In the months following the Republican takeover of the United States Congress in 1994, the press relentlessly attacked the Speaker of the House of Representatives, Congressman Newt Gingrich of Georgia. They sought to make him unpopular and they succeeded. Among the techniques used to accomplish this task was *word twisting*. On April 2, 1995, journalist John Cochran did a story on Speaker Gingrich for *This Week With David Brinkley*. The following is from that report:

John Cochran: "Doubts stem from ethical questions surrounding a college course he used to teach and, of course, his book deal with Rupert Murdoch. Democrat Barney Frank led the attack on the book contract. He also blames Gingrich for much of the mean-spiritedness of American politics."

Congressman Barney Frank: "More than any other single figure in American politics, Newt Gingrich is responsible for the vicious tone, because he succeeded with it, and success breeds imitation."

John Cochran to audience: "We asked Gingrich about Frank's remarks."

John Cochran to Speaker Gingrich: "He says you are a remarkable leader in some ways but that you are divisive. Is that fair?"

Speaker Gingrich replies: "Yes, I'm leading a revolution and he is on the other side of it."

The trick works like this. First Cochran tells us that Representative Barney Frank attributes a mean-spirited atmosphere to Speaker Gingrich. Then Cochran tells the audience that he asked Speaker Gingrich about the Barney Frank accusation. But Cochran actually asked Gingrich a different question. He changed and softened what Congressman Frank said and asked

Gingrich if he [Gingrich] were divisive. And Gingrich seems to be answering the question, "Are you responsible for instigating partisan divisions on the issues?" Thus, journalist Cochran makes Gingrich appear to be admitting to contributing to mean-spirited politics, when he is actually admitting to something considerably less pernicious - winning political battles!

Word twisting often follows a false logic similar to the sophistry of fast-talking con artists. That is, journalists use tricky language to create a false *impression* and then talk as if the *impression* were a proven fact. The press coverage of the Republican Contract With America is a good example. In 1994 Republicans running for Congress promised to bring ten items up for a vote in the House, if voters gave them control of the Congress. These were old Republican proposals that the Democrats had refused to allow to come to a vote when they were in control of the House of Representatives. This Republican promise became known as the Contract with America.

In the first one hundred days of the 104th Congress, the Republicans brought all ten Contract items up for a vote as promised. Some of the items were voted down by the House of Representatives. Other items passed and were sent on to the United States Senate for consideration. Some of those items were passed on to Democratic President Clinton for signature. He ultimately signed over half into law and vetoed the rest. The Republican-led House of Representatives did what they promised: they brought up the ten items up for a vote.

Congressional Republicans could go into the 1996 election claiming, "Promises made, promises kept." Democrats were not pleased and claimed that the Contract with America was a failure because all of it did not become law. Democrats accused Republicans of not keeping their word. Democrats did it by twisting the words "promise to bring up for a vote" into "promise to become law." The press picked up this twist virtually intact. But they were indirect. They described the Contract as a "political dud" and the Republican Congress as "not measuring up." Such false judgements surely lead some news consumers to believe that the Republican House of Representative failed to bring up the Contract for vote and thus did not keep their word.

Abusive Use of Vague Sources

Attributing statements to a vague source is a common practice in everyday conversation and usually does no harm.[14] Someone might say something like, "It has been proven that people don't get AIDS from saliva." Notice the statement did not say who did the proving. This form of speech is called the passive voice. The passive voice is the grammatical construction which allows the speaker to refer to an activity without identifying who is performing the activity.

People learn the passive voice at an early age. Consider the child who has broken a vase or dinner plate. He might say something like, "It got broke," suggesting that he had nothing to do with the deed. This is a slick answer because the child does not overtly deny he that he broke it, while inviting his parents to believe that someone else broke it. Grown people use the passive voice for the same dishonest reasons. Some of those people are journalists.

An example of the abusive use of passive voice comes from some reports on Central American conflicts in the 1980s. Many civilians were killed by unknown assailants in that Cold War conflict. In Liberal and progressive circles it was believed that those political killings were the work of right-wing Conservative forces. The Liberal press shared the belief that the so-called right wing was responsible for "death squad" activity. So broadcast journalists usually said something like, "The killings are believed to be carried out by forces of the right wing."[15] The passive voice allows the reporter to avoid identifying who is doing the believing. Thus he can suggest that this "right wing" is solely responsible for political killings without the burden of producing any evidence.

Journalists can also mislead the thinking of news consumers by using a vague source. It may work like this. Suppose an imaginary reporter from XYZ Evening News states, "Scientists have shown that acid rain is destroying the forests and lakes of the northeast United States." The statement is vague because it leaves unanswered who is saying this. Was it the ten-year NAPAP study conducted by two thousand scientists? Was it a rump report from an environmental activist group? Or a drinking buddy of the reporter? The impression is projected to news consumers that all scientists agree with the statement when that is not true at all.

Ringer Sources

Have you ever wondered where journalists get those experts on global warming, education, economics and acid rain? The interesting thing about the expert opinion that shows up on the television news is that it always seems to support the Liberal point of view. In fact, journalists have a definite preference for sources which fit their Liberal beliefs.[16] It's not difficult for journalists to find an expert to tell them what they want to hear. Such an expert is commonly called **a ringer**.

According to my dictionary, a ringer is "one who enters a competition under false representations." A ringer expert, then, is one who speaks under false pretenses. Partisans routinely use experts under false pretenses in an effort to influence public opinion. Partisans are motivated to ignore all experts, except those with which they agree. (See chapter three.) Journalists also succumb to the same partisan temptation.

That is, journalists present quotes from experts on controversial issues as if all other experts in the field were in agreement, when that is not the case. This is a false representation. Expert opinion found on the news is more representative of journalist opinion than expert knowledge on the disputed issue. By falsely representing expert testimony, journalists create the news image that Liberal opinion is proven fact.

A good example of false news image was revealed by a study of nuclear reporting conducted by the Center for Media and Public Affairs.[17] The study showed that the expert opinion aired on the evening news did not reflect the consensus of specialists in the energy field. What the evening news did reflect was the consensus of the opinion of journalists reporting on nuclear energy. Like a ventriloquist making it look as if the dummy were actually speaking, leading science journalists used experts to make it appear as if the whole scientific community were actually speaking.

Journalists also misrepresent public opinion. Yes, they correctly report the public opinion polls, leaving aside the question of the correctness of the polls. It is when journalists include anecdotal "man in the street" interviews in television news stories that the press creates a false image of public opinion. That is, the selection of voices from the people is more representative of opinion in the journalistic community than the community at large. With little effort, journalists can find somebody someplace to say whatever a journalist might want them to say. The following is a good example.

During the 1990 Persian Gulf War, the three major networks -- ABC, CBS and NBC -- jeered U.S. policy. Fifty-nine percent of all sources aired by the networks were critical of United States policy in the war. At this time public support for the war was over ninety percent. Elite journalists were doing something more than holding up a mirror to reality. Clearly the anti-war tenor of the war reporting reflected the perspectives of journalists themselves and not that of the American public. "Anti-war" opinion could not have been greater than 8 percent, since the highwater mark for support of the war was 92 percent. However, the "anti-war" activists must share that 8 percent with the Genghis Khan types who thought President Bush should "nuke them till they glow in the dark." The "anti-war" sources were given a disproportionate share of air time, thus creating the false image that many Americans were against the war.

Elite journalists reflexively employ verbal spin. They are masters at saying things without appearing to do so. They have high linguistic skills, finding it easy to suggest, insinuate, give out hints and drop cues in a presumptuous effort to insert *correct* opinion into the news. It is this partisan spin that really makes television news offensive to non-Liberal viewers.

SUMMARY

By and large, politics in this country is an advertising contest between warring political camps seeking to sway public opinion one way or the other. The weapon of choice in this information war is "spin." Spin is the presentation of information designed to influence public opinion.

During political disputes each side tries to put its own self-serving spin on the issue in question. That's expected. It's called politics. Journalists are supposed to report on this public relations war, not participate in it. However, the Liberal press actively shapes the flow of information reaching the public in a manner that helps the Democratic political party.

It is important to note that leading journalists don't usually engage in obvious partisan persuasion. They do not employ propagandistic harangues designed to win people to the cause of Liberal Democrats. They would be fools to do so. The ineffectiveness of these techniques is well known. Years of research dating back to the Second World War illustrates the futility of such heavy-handed efforts. While people resist being lectured at, many can be influenced by subtle hints and cues of spin.

Thus, what we see in the news is this subtler form of persuasion. Journalists feed news consumers selected pieces of the truth and suggest how those pieces should fit together. Those suggestions are embedded into the context of the news. Suggestions get there by the very way the news is gathered, produced and presented. **What news journalists choose to tell and how they tell it, unavoidably suggests how that news should be understood.** Put another way, **the capacity to decide what becomes news and how that news is told, is the capacity to influence public opinion.** It is those little contextual messages in news stories that move public opinion. Thus the Liberal press tries to *influence public opinion merely by manipulating the contextual suggestions in the news*. But like any other advertising effort, sometimes it works and sometimes it doesn't.

DISCUSSION

My primary motivation for writing this chapter was to show how ridiculously easy it is for the elite journalists to slip partisan messages into the contextual framework of news productions. It was clear that political bias in the news was linked to implied messages, unspoken suggestions, subtext and the unacknowledged assumptions of journalists. Thus, it was clear that spin equals bias. The problem was to discover and describe the source of spin and how it gets into the news.

There is a problem with my use of academic research. Since most academics are Liberals or Radicals, the authors of these studies may not approve of how I use their work. The political prejudice that I discuss also extends to the university. Since the publishing of Edith Efron's book, **The News Twisters**, in 1972, Liberal academics have fought against even the very idea of Liberal bias in the news. In fact many have argued for a Conservative bias put there by the capitalistic ownership of news outlets. So, I use their work as an attorney might quote from a hostile witness. In any case I take full responsibility for my interpretation of the academic work presented above.

One may quibble with my interpretation of the data, but a few things seem clear: (1) *Journalists are in the public opinion business.* They actually try to influence political outcomes. (2) Journalists employ the subtle and indirect spin suggestions described above. (3) There is growing evidence that people are highly attuned to contextual suggestions in the news. And there is evidence that the techniques do work.

END NOTES

(1) See page xiii of **FDR's Splendid Deception** by Hugh Gregory Gallagher, published by Dead, Mead & Company in New York in 1985.

(2) See the piece, *Who Killed Privacy*, by Correspondent Bernard Goldberg presented on the CBS program "Eye to Eye" for August 24, 1995.

(3) See, *Who Killed Privacy?*, by Correspondent Goldberg

(4) See **FDR's Splendid Deception** by Hugh Gregory Gallagher

(5) Read the section titled "Minimal Effects Revisited" starting on page 116 of **News That Matters** by Shanto Iyengar and Donald R. Kinder, published by The University of Chicago Press, Chicago, Illinois, in 1987.

(6) It is characteristic of the prejudiced style of thinking to promote self-serving fiction as proven fact. Political fictions are the natural outgrowth of partisan conflicts. Fictions support the in-group version of reality. Some of these political fictions serve a political purpose. They tell of the good deeds of the political in-group and the bad deeds of the opposition.

See the book, **Does Mass Communication Change Public Opinion After All**? by James B. Lemert, published by Nelson-Hall in Chicago Illinois, for a discussion of what Professor Lemert calls "situation definitions," which is what I am calling "political fictions."

(7) Journalists' use of the words "cut" and "savings" is actually a bit muddled, except when it really mattered. In October, 1995, NBC's "Nightly News" referred to Republican-sponsored budget cuts as "savings." After January, 1996, the press pretty much uniformly used the word "savings." It was during the heated battle in December 95 and January 96 that many in the television press insisted that it was *fact* that Republicans were cutting Medicare. Journalists associated the word "cut" with the Republicans just enough to give many news consumers the idea that Republicans were actually cutting Medicare.

(8) See pages 176 to 187 of *The Agenda-Setting Function of Mass Media.* by Maxwell E. McCombs and Donald L. Shaw published in Volume 36 of **Public Opinion Quarterly**.

(9) See pages 29 to 31 of **The Mass Media in Campaign '84**, edited by Michael J. Robinson and Austin Ranney published by the American Enterprise Institute, Washington, D.C. It should be noted that Professor Robinson does not think there is any Liberal bias in the news *of any consequence!* Likely he would not approve of what I am doing with his study of the 1984 presidential campaign.

(10) The word "priming" comes from the operation of firearms. A *primer* is a device for used to ignite the main explosive charge. Inset in the base of a 38 or 45 caliber cartridge is a little circle. That little circular device is the primer for the cartridge. When the firing pin strikes it, the primer ignites the powder, which expels the bullet at the other end of the cartridge. The idea behind priming people is similar.

(11) Read chapter seven of **News That Matters** by Shanto Iyengar and Donald R. Kinder, published by The University of Chicago Press, located in Chicago, Illinois, in 1987.

(12) Read chapter seven of **News That Matters.**

(13) Likely these academics would not agree with my evaluations. See the discussion section above.

(14) A **source** is *a source of information*; it can be a person or a document. There are times when the source is not revealed, often for a good reason. Sources of news about governmental wrongdoing might very well evaporate if their names were used. There is ongoing controversy over the use of unnamed sources. But journalists often make vague references to sources. In many cases they are not "protecting" a source but referring to a false consensus. This can be an abusive practice.

(15) On March 26, 1990, National Public Radio aired a report on the death of a Central American Catholic Bishop. An NPR reporter said that, "forces from the right wing are believed to be responsible."

(16) See the section *Searching for Sources* in chapter three of **The Media Elite**, by S. Robert Lichter, Stanley Rothman and Linda S. Lichter, published by Adler & Adler, Bethesda, Maryland, in 1986. The authors focused on four areas: welfare reform, consumer protection, the environment and nuclear energy. "Where do the media elite turn for reliable information? On welfare reform, liberal sources predominate over conservative ones. On consumer issues they look to Ralph Nader, the public interest movement and liberal activist groups. On pollution and the environment, they select activist environmental groups and, once again, liberal leaders. On nuclear energy, anti-nuclear sources are the most popular."

(17) See the study, *Nuclear News* by S. Robert Lichter, Stanley Rothman, Robert W. Rycroft and Linda S. Lichter of the Center for Media and Public Affairs, May, 1986.

Chapter 8

SCANDALMONGERING

One of the good features of democracy is that partisans don't routinely kill off their enemies. However assassinating the character of political opponents is standard practice. In that effort, partisans use "dirt," real or imagined, to bring down the opposition. When politicians dig up dirt on their enemies, it's called *opposition research*. When journalists dig up dirt on their enemies, it's called *investigative reporting*. I call it *scandalmongering*, no matter who engages in the activity. All scandalmongers use the old muckraking tactic.[1]

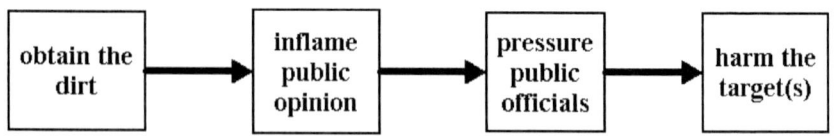

First, scandal promoting partisans (*the accusers*) dig up dirt on enemy partisans (*the targets*). Dirt is information about an allegedly improper activity. The information may or may not be valid and the activity may or may not actually be improper. Then the accusers self-righteously denounce the targets and declare them unfit for public office. They try to get the attention of the press in order to distribute the dirt to a mass audience. The accusers hope that public knowledge of the dirt will inspire citizens to pressure their public officials to take harmful action against enemy targets.

The press plays a key role. It is the medium (the media) through which accusers must publicize the (allegedly) improper behavior of enemy targets. Likewise, damage control teams working on behalf of the target must also go through the press in order to defend the target. If the press favors the target, it can make it all but impossible for the accusers to distribute attack information to a mass audience in a timely manner. On the other hand, if the press favors the scandal promoters, the press can facilitate efforts to distribute the dirt to the public.

While not all-powerful, the press can focus public attention on the alleged wrongdoing of almost any political enemy. And at the same time, they can distract public attention away from the actual wrongdoing of almost any political friend. Even when circumstances force the press to cover the wrongdoing of a political friend, journalists can always blunt the public relations damage.

In the battle for public opinion, competing partisans often fight over what is and is not a scandal. Their motivations color their perceptions. Scandal promoters and their supporters are motivated to perceive dreadful wrongdoing. Scandal targets and their supporters don't want to perceive any scandal. Targets conclude (often correctly) that the accusers were simply out to "get" them.

I once called a radio talk show and tried to compare the news coverage of a Republican scandal with the coverage of a Democratic scandal. The Liberal-minded host told me I was comparing apples and oranges. He said, in essence, that the really bad things Republicans did during the Iran/Contra Scandal can't be compared with the unimportant little missteps that dethroned Democratic Speaker of the House of Representatives, James Wright of Texas.

After that exchange of perceptions, I sought a definition based on *fact*, not on partisan *perceptions*. I consulted my dictionary. It said that a scandal is a "loss of or damage to reputation caused by actual or apparent violation of morality or propriety." Note that the alleged perpetrator may be innocent or guilty; it does not matter. Note also that a scandal involves a loss of "reputation" due to the public *perception* of improper behavior, again not the actual behavior. However there's a problem with this definition.

It's difficult to verify a loss of reputation. In order to avoid the influence of partisan perceptions, a scandal should be verifiable by an independent observer. Thus, a scandal should be defined in terms of tangible events. The target needs to suffer some sort of tangible loss.

In summary, for a scandal to occur, the following events must take place: (1) Partisans publicly accuse a target of impropriety, (2) A sizable segment of the public must believe that a flagrant impropriety occurred, and (3) The target or an associate must be forced to suffer a tangible loss.

An **impropriety** is just about anything that can be construed to be improper. Breaking a law or a moral code can be judged improper. Lying to citizens or using forbidden words can also be improper. If the target has not committed any real transgression, the accusers can invent an impropriety tailored for the occasion. The alleged impropriety is often experienced by the accusers as a kind of political crime. That crime often occurs when enemy partisans win an election.

A **sizable segment** of the public is not easy to define. However, I think it has to be greater than 20 percent. Each political grouping - Conservative, Libertarian, Liberal, Populist and uninvolved - accounts for about 20 percent of the population. Most Liberals are in a permanent state of outrage over leading Conservatives and vice versa. That's the natural state of partisan politics. A sizable segment ought to be greater than the total number of Conservatives or the total number of Liberals. Therefore, a threshold number might be, say, 30 percent. To reach the 30 percent would require the entire Liberal segment, for instance, plus 10 percent from the Conservatives, Libertarians and Populists.

A **tangible loss** can range from a public wrist slapping to the loss of job or time in jail. The target might be forced to pay hundreds of thousands of dollars to lawyers in order to defend himself in a court of law. Or the target may otherwise have his life unpleasantly disrupted. The loss might be taken by a close associate of the target.

A **scandal event** is any event connected with an attempted scandal or scandal promotion as well as the actual scandal. Accuser scandal events may be staged. Such pseudo-events would not occur if there were no news organization to cover them. In fact, it should be noted that it is exceedingly difficult to stage events without willing accomplices in the press. A scandal event may also be an real event. A real event is one that would occur even if there were no journalist to report it. Official investigations and court trials are real events. Actual wrongdoing is a scandal event. Actions taken by the accusers to bring down the target are real events. And whatever steps the target takes to control the public relations damage are also real events.

THE TYPICAL SUCCESSFUL SCANDAL

When the press favors the accusers, scandals tend to achieve some success and unfold in similar fashion. First, there is *the promotional phase*. Political partisans are always trying to promote a scandal -- any scandal -- to bring down the opposition on the cheap. Partisans are always looking for a media opportunity to inflame public opinion against their political enemies. Actual evidence of wrongdoing is not relevant to this activity. However, many attempted scandals never get out of this stage.

Scandal promoters present all manner of rumor, innuendo and outright fiction, as well as actual facts, in their efforts to destroy an enemy target. Any behavior that can be construed as an *impropriety* is fair game. Even the appearance of wrongdoing is considered highly relevant by accusers out to harm the competition. Doing their best to install an easy proof of wrongdoing, accusers claim that all such information is important, relevant and likely true.

Meanwhile the target and his allies work hard to control the public relations damage. They do the reasonable thing. They develop a strategy to limit the worst effects of the scandal. This activity is known as damage control. The target and his friends will try to counter the flow of damaging information to the public. Like the defense team in a criminal trial, they are out to destroy the credibility of the accusers. Even if there is actual evidence of impropriety, the damage control team will still say that the accusation is not credible. They tell people that the evidence is biased and tainted.

If that doesn't work, damage control may claim that the evidence is riddled with mind-numbing details in which nobody is interested. If the target is obviously guilty, damage control may claim a statute of limitations on the impropriety. Or they may claim that target *impropriety* is not important. They will sternly claim it takes hard evidence of recent criminal wrongdoing to raise the scandal flag high enough to drive the target from public office!

Scandal promoters often fail in their attempts. However, sometimes they convince enough people that the target behaved improperly. If the accusers continue to play their cards right, scandal promoters can force the target to suffer some kind of loss. As the accusers engage in pious public tisking, the scandal enters what I call the *Witch Hunt Phase*. Emboldened by their success, the accusers now seek to hunt down targets of opportunity and punish them in the full view of the public, and thus maximize public relations damage to opposing political forces.

Public opinion gains are the real payoff. It is during the Witch Hunt Phase that accusers can visit real political damage on the target. And with any luck the accusers will be able to smear the entire political party of the target. It may be possible to silence the enemy political party for a period of time. If a scandal is played right, accusers can convert the public outrage to political power, thus avoiding the tedium of a democratic electoral process.

That's why the target and his allies desperately try to minimize the Witch Hunt Phase. There are several possibilities. Perhaps there is an opportunity to engage in a successful cover-up. Or the target may "feed someone to the wolves" satisfying the public appetite for some sort of loss. In any case, the idea is to bring the Witch Hunt Phase to a speedy close. Perhaps the accusers will fail to make the attack information public in the most damaging fashion, presenting the target with an opportunity to mount a successful public relations counterattack. Or the target may upstage the accusers and release enough damaging information early in the scandal cycle.

Republican President Ronald Reagan did exactly that in 1987. President Reagan was able to minimize the worst effects of scandalmongering by releasing the worst information soon after the scandal broke. Remember that the Republican President was accused of trading arms to Iran in order to free hostages in the Middle East and then funneling the profits to people fighting the Communists in Central America. It became known as the Iran/Contra Scandal.[2] Before this scandal had run its course, several people lost their jobs with the Reagan Administration. Some were actually brought to trial for their Iran-Contra crimes. Lots of people believed in the alleged wrongdoing and there were plenty of accusers.

However, it was not as bad as it could have been. President Reagan was able to maintain credibility with the public because his version of the scandal remained intact. Subsequent Congressional and press investigations turned up little that was new. The televised hearings, staged by Congressional Democrats to indirectly attack President Reagan, backfired. The primo target, LtCol. Oliver North won the public relations battle by his stunning television performance in his spiffy Marine Corps uniform and military bearing. That reversal of public opinion fortunes took the steam out of the political attack launched by Democrats and their accomplices in the Washington press corps. The conclusion of the hearings marked the end of the Witch Hunt phase for the Iran-Contra Scandal.

Even though there are no more witches to hunt down and punish, a successful scandal goes on. At this point the scandal enters a *"Bloody Shirt" Phase*.[3] While there are no more targets to destroy, the accusers are able to still stir up some public animosity against the enemy political party. The object is to inhibit the opposition, end risky debate and score political points with the public. The Bloody Shirt Phase ends when the accusers and their friends are no longer able to squeeze public relations profits from the old scandal.

Watergate is a good example of a scandal with a long Bloody Shirt Phase. Long after all the Watergate conspirators were sent to prison, Democrats, with the help of the elite media, effected public relations losses against the Republicans. Even today the old Watergate reporters still bask in the glory of their accomplishment: bringing down a very popular and competent Republican president.

However, when the press favors the target as it has done with President Clinton, the flow of scandal events as described above can be disrupted, severely disabling the scandalmongers. As I have shown in the chapter on spin, the press has great power to influence the way many people think about events, including scandal events. When the press is dominated by one political faction, as it is now, it can frame scandal events to favor the target. In this case, scandal promoters need to go around the press to get at public opinion.

SCANDAL PERSPECTIVES

Typically the accuser and target are opposing partisans who have conflicting perceptions of each other (as well as many other issues and situations). Each views the other as unscrupulous, cruel, power hungry and inferior. Accusers and their sympathizers perceive corrupt politicians caught in the act of sordid wrongdoing, while the target perceives accusers as callous partisans out to destroy decent people for personal gain.

The Accuser Attitude. The attitude towards scandals is driven by the partisan biases described in chapter three. Thinking that they are non-partisan, accusers view themselves to be above the political fray. They fancy themselves to be humble seekers of truth and justice. Accusers apprehend a civic duty to hunt down and punish wrongdoers. Whistle blowers are perceived as heros. Accusers see themselves engaged in a righteous cause, not as peddlers of political dirt. Only enemy out-groups do that.

Accusers perceive serious character flaws in enemy partisans. It is this perceived lack of character that disqualifies the enemy target from holding high political office. Some partisans think it is scandalous for their opponents to even be in politics. Accusers often see the current scandal as only the latest example of a long history of wrongdoing.

Thus guilt of improper activity is easily determined. Simple membership in a political out-group might be enough. Efforts by the target to defend himself may be taken as proof of wrongdoing. If the target tries to discover the hidden motivations of the accusers, that may be perceived as a dirty trick suggesting guilt. The earnestness of the accuser may be enough, on its own, to declare guilt.

The accusers, being dead sure that the target has engaged in wrongdoing, are insensitive to any unfair treatment suffered by the target. As accusers see it, the target is surely guilty of something. The target is often guilty of defeating the accuser in a previous political contest. That defeat may be seen by the accusers as a kind of political crime. As the accusers see it, the target has already forfeited his rights to a fair hearing by his high crimes. Thus, the accusers display little interest in fair play for the target.

The Target Attitude. The target and his supporters view the situation quite differently, of course. They view themselves as simply trying to make the world a better place. The targets perceive the accusers as unprincipled demagogues, callously out to destroy good people for selfish political advantage. Seeing himself as the victim of a smear campaign, the target typically feels that his rights are being trampled. Responding in kind, the target will aggressively question the partisan motives of the accusers. The target is often right in his perception of the motives and political agenda of the accusers. With a sense of being wronged, the target will demand the right to a fair hearing.

Thus, factors other than the alleged wrongdoing become important. The target and his supporters perceive the political combat as the critical element of any scandal events. Targets explain scandal events in terms of the give and take of partisan politics. Targets will tell people that the accusers are just trying to create a political distraction. They will claim that getting the people's work done is much more important than any scandal story.

Perceiving the scandal allegations as a tempest in a teapot, the target and his friends try to discourage interest in any of the scandal events. They will tell people that the scandal stories are dull, boring or old news. Target supporters may try to convince people that information about the scandal is insanely complicated. Even if all this damage control fails, targets and their supporters are not deterred.

If improprieties obviously happened, target and friends will still try to find a way to claim that it does not matter. A damage control team may claim that the voters have already rendered their verdict on the target. That is, if the target has been elected to office, the American people have already made their judgement about any improprieties. Or the target may admit that some little mistakes were made and that the mistakes may have had unfortunate consequences, but he should still remain in office. A guilty target may claim to have gone through some transforming experience and is not the same person who previously made mistakes, so he should still remain in office.

Even though the target is proven guilty, friends and allies still perceive him as a good person who accidently did something wrong for entirely understandable reasons. If the target is forced out of office, his supporters will perceive that event as an unfortunate tragedy that overtook a really good person.

PRESS COVERAGE OF SCANDALS

A scandal is a form of information combat not unlike the one that occurs during a court trial. There, prosecutors accuse defendants of serious wrongdoing and present evidence (information) to support their claims. The prosecutor will organize and present the evidence in a way that will put the defendant in the worst possible light. The defendant presents evidence (information) designed to undercut the prosecution case. The defendant will engage in various stratagems to control the damage from the prosecution attack. In a court trial, prosecutor and defendant battle for the opinion of the jury. In the court of public opinion, scandal accusers and targets conduct a similar battle for opinion. There is one important difference.

In the political arena, accusers and targets can't talk directly to the electorate as lawyers talk to the jury. Accusers and targets are forced to talk to journalists who, in turn, talk to a mass audience. That is, accusers and targets must go through the press in order to communicate to the American people. This gives extraordinary power to the press establishment. Journalists are in the catbird seat. While not all-powerful, the press can influence public opinion. Employing the techniques of political spin, the press can focus public attention on almost any accusation of wrongdoing against any Republican, no matter how insignificant the alleged wrongdoing. And the press can limit the public relations damage to any Democrat, no matter what his crime. The Liberal press achieves its partisan political objectives by constructing one news image for Democratic scandals and a different news image for Republican scandals. The following paragraphs outline the major traits of that news image.

Covering Republican Targets

When a Republican is the target, the Liberal press assumes the accuser attitude. Before any scandal event occurs, the Liberal press presumes Republicans guilty. The partisan perception is that Republicans can't gain and keep political power without committing political crimes. Because they are primed to believe the worst of Republicans, only a whiff of a scandal can energize the Liberal wing of the press establishment. (The "October Surprise" attempted scandal is a good example.)

Journalists chase the story with the enthusiasm of a "crusading district attorney" out to reform a corrupt city government. Journalists fully intend to haul Republican targets before the court of public opinion and punish them for their political crimes. Throwing the full weight of their investigative power into the hunt, Liberal journalists aggressively seek every scrap of scandal information about the Republican target. (Scandal information can be anything from bad grades in college to obstruction of justice.) Of course, there is no statute of limitations for digging up dirt on Republicans. Anything in the past of any Republican is fair game.

1. The Standard of Conduct - When Republicans are the target, the elite press employs a very high standard of conduct for public officials. Almost any transgression is defined as improper. Thus, lying can be grounds for the press to extract a public relations punishment from a Republican. Womanizing can be used to deny high political office to a Republican. (In 1995, Robert Packwood was run out the United States Senate for what amounted to *attempted womanizing*.) The standard for judging Republicans is not only high, it is also wide. Republican targets are held responsible for the behavior of anybody connected with them. Thus, if a staffer behaves improperly, the press will smear the Republican target with the ancillary scandal.

2. The Standard of Proof - While holding Republicans to a high standard of conduct, the Liberal press employs *a low standard of proof* of wrongdoing. The journalistic requirement for proving Republican guilt is easy to meet. The words and images in the news provide good reason to believe that many journalists view leading Republicans as mean-spirited low life. Thus, it takes little actual evidence to suggest that a Republican target has behaved improperly. The stature of the Democratic accuser may be enough. The seriousness of the accusations may be enough. Target efforts to control the public relations damage may be itself be taken as evidence of guilt. If a Republican cover-up is uncovered, it will be taken as a crime on its own merits, even if proof of impropriety is never actually found.

Since the Liberal press has already judged Republican targets guilty, it is not necessary to give them a fair hearing in the court of public opinion. It is up to Republican targets to prove themselves innocent, and the Liberal press is not going to make that task very easy. Interviews with Republican targets become blood sport, with bully boy journalists vying with each other to land "the killer question" and knock the target out of politics.

3. Connecting the Scandal Dots - Connecting the dots is what journalists routinely do for a living. Journalists tell stories. Connecting the dots is at the core of the journalistic art. They gather some facts and connect those facts (dots) into a narrative story. In a real sense journalists always go beyond the facts; they must, to get the narrative story. Thus, different stories could be told using the same sources of information. Journalists have a lot of latitude in deciding when they have enough information to tell a story and what story to tell.

An important part of telling a scandal story is to judge the seriousness of the (alleged) scandal offenses. When covering Republicans, almost anything that can be construed as an impropriety is judged to be serious. That is, journalists typically go beyond the facts to suggest that Republicans may have done something improper. Elite journalists often leap over the information and report that the Republican target is guilty of what amounts in some sense to, *crimes against society*. The very political existence of a Republican is often the actual crime.

Whether journalists have the facts or not, they constantly suggest that a serious Republican scandal lurks in the information shadows. They sternly claim that the various scraps of scandal information "raise serious questions" about "possible" wrongdoing. In this charged partisan atmosphere, journalists become hypersensitive to Republican missteps. Thus, an inadvertent inconsistency becomes a purposeful lie. Ordinary differences between spoken words and behavior become cynical hypocrisy. A common slip of the tongue becomes one more sign of incompetence. Any political corner cut becomes a serious ethical lapse.

4. In other words, **journalists hype the scandal story**, blowing it out of proportion. A scandal story that belongs on page 11 is put on page one with big headlines. Journalists employ the techniques of spin to create a larger image of wrongdoing than can be justified by the facts in hand. News consumers are told that the scandal story is very important. The hype itself plants the suggestion that Republicans pose a danger to society.

5. Thus, **a "good versus evil" theme dominates news products.** Scandal events are explained in terms of improper Republican behavior. News stories may become morality plays with accuser Democrats as selfless heroes, while Republican targets are cast as the villains. News products validate the credibility of the accusers. The accusers are presented as heroes. For instance, the press turned Professor Anita Hill into a brave pillar of society during the attempted scandal against Justice Clarence Thomas in 1991.

This "good versus evil" theme reflects the partisan bias common to most elite newsrooms. Remember that leading journalists are about 89 percent Liberal Democrat. The partisan bias of a Liberal press is characterized by an "us versus them" attitude, with Democrats as *us* and Republicans as *them*. This thematic treatment indirectly urges news consumers to believe that Republican targets are guilty of wrongdoing and are unfit for public office. Remember that planting suggestions in the context of the news is the primary technique for inducing a partisan spin on the news.

6. News products plant suggestions of Republican wrongdoing. - Even though journalists may not have the smoking gun story, they will still find ways to suggest that the Republican target has behaved improperly. There are many ways to accomplish the task. The "good versus evil" theme is one way. Another is using headlines and the first sentence to frame the subsequent story in the minds of news consumers. Leads suggest how the accompanying news production should be understood. And leads to Republican scandal stories typically suggest wrongdoing.

News products are peppered with loaded scandal words. When Republicans are the target, journalists may seize accusatory questions they hope will uncover Republicans wrongdoing. Attack questions typically come from the point of view of a Liberal Democrat. Attack questions are augmented with loaded words like, "self-damaging," "complicity," "shocking," "criminal," "shredding," "wrongdoing," "lying" and "corruption."

News products about Republican targets are somber in tone, which helps to suggest target guilt. Journalists with long faces tell news consumers that the charges are very serious. They will soberly pick through the maybe facts as if reporting from the scene of an atrocity. Journalists will find ways to communicate to the viewing audience that they are revolted by Republican targets. They may employ non-verbal cues like a roll of the eyes, an intake of breath or a dismissive wave of the hand.

7. Thus, the partisan motives of accuser Democrats are not important. That's because the Liberal press believes that their fellow Democrats act out of good motives. This is not surprising. Partisans typically attribute good motives to other in-group members. Statements made by Democrats are very often taken at face value. (Republican sources are treated with suspicion.) Any partisan motives of the accuser Democrats are deemed not to be newsworthy, not an important part of *the story*. It is the "improper" behavior of Republican targets which is the real story.

8. Judging News Value. After journalists investigate a scandal event they must decide on its news value. Only a solid suspicion of wrongdoing is required to rush accusatory news products into print or put them on the air. It is deemed good journalism to quickly get the scandal information out to the public. Indeed, elite news organizations act as if they were performing a public service. Democrats are given a convenient sounding board to get their scandal promotions out to a mass audience. That is, Democrats are allowed unopposed free air time to attack Republicans, with journalists rarely challenge Democrats on their so-called facts. It becomes common practice for the Liberal press to air "*maybe Republicans are guilty*" stories. The so-called "October Surprise" is a good example of a maybe story.

9. The Resulting News Image. The dominant impression left by accusatory news stories is that target Republicans did something improper and unacceptable. Not every news story exhibits all the above coverage traits. However, enough of the traits surface during the coverage of any scandal or an attempted scandal to paint an image of Republican wrongdoing. And that image of *serious wrongdoing* can drive public opinion. Even when there is no actual evidence of wrongdoing, news products may still be crafted to <u>suggest</u> that serious wrongdoing actually occurred.

Covering Democratic Targets

When leading Democrats are the scandal target, journalists adopt the target attitude. When journalists switch from reporting on Republican targets to Democratic targets, they undergo an amazing metamorphosis. Crusading watchdogs out to reform society suddenly become picky and legalistic. Gone are the grave concerns about "the people's right to know." New information no longer "raises questions" about "possible" wrongdoing. Gone are the aggressive information vigilantes bringing the bad guys to justice. Gone is the excitement of getting the big story of corrupt politicians in high places. There is a sudden lack of eagerness to go after scandal information. Journalists find some excuse to drag their investigative feet. When the press finally gets around to covering the story, they will try to release the information in the most harmless fashion.

A common and effective way to render the scandal harmless is to frame the story in terms of the usual political combat, Republicans fighting Democrats. Rather than the "high crimes and misdemeanors" angle they used on Republicans during Watergate and Iran/Contra, the press frames Democratic scandals in terms of partisan combat. It is well known that reporting scandal events as "business as usual" does not pack much public opinion punch. People expect politicians to behave like, well, politicians.

Of course, there is a statute of limitations for digging up dirt on Democrats. As the coverage of the Whitewater Scandal demonstrated, Liberal journalists will claim that improper activity from the distant past is not relevant. Consider this comment made by Anchor Dan Rather aired on the CBS Evening News, March 24, 1994, "President Clinton takes his Whitewater fight back campaign to the nation, tonight in a broadcast news conference. Accusations about the *old* Arkansas savings and loan deal keep coming up. [emphasis added] Some of the nastiest yet, came from a Republican this afternoon." Notice that Mr. Rather is <u>suggesting</u> that the improper activity does not matter because it occurred before President Clinton was elected to office. Notice also that Rather is accusing the Republicans of being nasty.

1. The Standard of Conduct. Elite journalists adopt a very lenient standard for judging the behavior of fellow Democrats. This is done by defining few transgressions as improper. Gone is the broad definition of wrongdoing. When a Democrat is the target, wrongdoing is defined very narrowly. Now the target must be convicted of a real crime in a real court to be deemed guilty of an impropriety.

Accusations against target Democrats are usually judged to be unimportant or frivolous. Democrats are usually given a pass on everything short of recent felony crimes. Improprieties like lying do not even register on the scale journalists use to judge the behavior of Democrats. Target Democrats are not held responsible for the behavior of anyone who works for them. Even when a close associate is found guilty of wrongdoing, journalists will still declare that the target has done nothing improper.

2. The Standard of Proof. While holding Democrats to a very low standard of conduct, the press employs a very high standard of proof of wrongdoing. Journalists get very legalistic. It takes a lot of evidence to prove a Democrat guilty of improper behavior. Pooh-poohing Republican accusations, journalists demand to be provided with *irrefutable evidence of serious high level wrongdoing*. The testimony of several henchpersons who directly witnessed the same wrongdoing might be enough proof. Until that is done, journalists constantly remind news consumers that the target Democrat is innocent, that the charges have not been proved. Now it takes something close to legal proof presented in a court of law for journalists to connect the scandal dots.

3. Connecting the Scandal Dots. Now, it's bad journalism to *go beyond the facts* to suggest target wrongdoing. And it's an easy journalism to accomplish. Journalists can always claim that the story is too complicated or that there is not enough evidence. Proof with mathematical certainty does not exist for any news story. And evidence is always incomplete and confusing. That's the nature of evidence. When covering Democrats, hard proof is required to tell a story of wrongdoing, and journalists encourage the news-consuming audience to do the same.

Thus, solid hard proof of serious wrongdoing is required for journalists to convert a theory of wrongdoing into factual news. And it is up to Republicans to go out and get that proof. And if that happens, surely the press would claim that the evidence is tainted and should be ignored because Republicans produced it. Journalists will resist connecting the dots. They will avoid telling the story of wrongdoing Democrats as long as possible.

4. Journalists deflate the story. Gone is the hypersensitivity to political missteps of the target. Slips of the target tongue rarely see the light of day. Hypocrisy may be praised as smart politics. Hard evidence of intent to deceive is required for a news organization to suggest that a Democrat is even lying, let alone committing a serious offense. Again, journalists employ the techniques of spin to deflate the story. The primary way to deflate a scandal story is to report it in a framework of "politics as usual."

5. The "Politics as Usual" Theme. Now scandal events are explained in terms of the usual political combat between Republicans and Democrats. Gone is the morality play of bad people caught in their own wrongdoing. Accuser whistle blowers are no longer presented as heroes. (Living Republicans aren't heroes.) There is a new story line and it's "politics as usual." There are several possible plot lines. Journalists may cast Democrats as innocent victims of nasty Republican attacks as Dan Rather did in the above quote. If it is not credible for journalists to discount the accusations against the Democrats, journalists may claim that Republicans are also guilty. Then the story line would become one of a corrupt political system in which all parties are tainted.

In this "politics as usual" framework, damage control efforts by Democratic targets is presented as understandable behavior. Even when the damage control becomes a cover-up, the Liberal press raises no flags. Journalists may scratch their heads and judge the cover-up to be bizarre behavior, but they will not condemn the Democrats. Some journalists have even had the chutzpa to say that the Whitewater Scandal was "a cover-up without a crime."

6. News Products Plant Suggestions of Innocence. News stories of Democratic targets take on a sympathetic tone. Journalists will ask the target how he is bearing up under the Republican onslaught. Of course, Liberal journalists will still find little ways to communicate to the viewing audience that they are revolted by Republican accusers. Story leads warn news consumers that the target Democrat has not been proven guilty of anything.

When Democrats are the target, journalists are on their good verbal behavior. Now the scandal news is noteworthy by the lack of attack questions and loaded words. Gone is the proliferation of scandal words like "shocking," "criminal," "shredding," "wrongdoing" and "lying." Gone are those head bashing questions journalists are so found of throwing at Republicans. Gone are the flame throwing journalists who try to singe the target at news conferences. Now questions are augmented with phrases like, "Well, er, you know I have to ask this." Now news conferences sound like they were staged by the Democratic National Committee.

It is very important to give Democratic targets a fair hearing. Since Democrats are presumed innocent, it is up to the accusers to make their case. The burden of proof is again on the Republicans. And the press is not going to make that job very easy. Democratic targets are given plenty of free and uncontested air time to answer the charges and launch personal attacks on Republicans. Interviews with Democratic targets are a love fest. Democrats are given a full public hearing to answer the charges.

7. Accuser Motives are Important. The partisan motives of accuser Republicans are very important. Since the allegations are seen by target Democrats and journalists as partisan politics, the partisan motives of the accuser Republicans are deemed to be newsworthy.

It is consistent with the target attitude, now adopted by the press, that the accusers have little credibility. In a court trial, the defense team always tries to ruin the credibility of the accusers. It is standard practice for anyone accused of anything whether they are innocent or guilty. It is what the damage control team always does. It is also standard practice in the press when Republicans are the accusers. The press treatment of the accusers in the various scandals and attempted scandals which have plagued Liberal Democratic President William Clinton provide some good examples.

8. Judging News Value. The standard for airing accusatory scandal stories becomes very high. When covering Democratic targets, the press adopts a very conservative attitude towards the craft of journalism. Journalists start throwing all kinds of hurdles in front of scandal stories. Scandal stories must be checked, rechecked and checked again to make sure the story is solid. Journalists will now agonize over the fairness of the coverage and the damage it might do to good people.

9. The Resulting News Image. Now the dominant impression from the scandal news is that target Democrats are innocent of any serious wrongdoing and voters should approve of them. Even when there is strong evidence of target wrongdoing, news products are shaped to <u>imply</u> that there is only an appearance of impropriety.

Not every news story exhibits all the biasing traits described above. However, enough of the traits are woven into the coverage of any scandal or an attempted scandal to shape an image of target innocence. The Liberal press will try to knock down the image of a scandal looming in the future. They will find ways to suggest that voters should approve of target Democrats.

PROFESSOR ANITA HILL VERSUS MS. PAULA JONES

It is instructive to compare the press coverage of Republican targets with that of Democratic targets. The contrasting press coverage illustrates the formidable capacity of partisan biases to distort the images that reach news consumers. In their daily work journalists must make a number of decisions and judgements. Those judgements profoundly shaped the news that ultimately reached the television set.

In the spring of 1991, Republican President George Bush nominated Judge Clarence Thomas to fill the vacancy left by retiring Justice Thurgood Marshall. As an African-American Conservative, Judge Thomas broke the Liberal stereotype of a Conservative as a racist. Horrified at the prospect of a black Conservative on the high court, the Liberal community fiercely opposed this nomination. During the confirmation hearings before the United States Senate, a former subordinate, Professor Anita Hill, came forward to accuse Thomas of sexual *misconduct.* The elite press pounced on the story, amplifying the partisan attack on Judge Thomas. The press covered Professor Hill with loving sympathy. However, her story was thin. The attempted scandal fizzled out and Judge Thomas was confirmed by the Senate to sit on the Supreme Court. No scandal.

At a February 11, 1994, news conference, Paula Jones accused President William Clinton of sexual harassment when he was governor of Arkansas and she was a clerk working for the Arkansas Industrial Development Commission. After failing to reach an out of court settlement, her lawyer filed a lawsuit against President Clinton. The press made it all but impossible for political Conservatives to promote the scandal. Scornful of Jones, leading journalists buried the story on the back pages. Finally the Jones team was able to extract a hefty settlement of some 850 thousand dollars form the Clinton camp making this a real scandal.

When Thomas was the target, the press assumed a prosecutorial attitude. At the initial news conference Hill accused Thomas of some vague "sexual misconduct." If guilty of that vague charge, Thomas would have been only guilty of talking dirty. But that did not stop the Liberal press from inflating the charges, judging them to be serious and making them sound like vicious sexual harassment.

But when favored Democrat William Jefferson Clinton strayed into the cross hairs of scandal, journalists set aside the prosecutorial attitude that characterized their coverage of the Thomas hearing. Assuming the attitude of defense attorney, the press presumed Clinton innocent and judged the charges to be frivolous. Even though Paula Jones actually accused President Clinton of sexual harassment, the elite press manufactured the impression that she had accused him only of some low-level sexual misconduct.

When Republican Thomas was the target, the press explained scandal events in terms of improper behavior. Journalists not only framed all news stories in terms of sexual harassment, the press led a national discussion on the subject. Of course, this "sexual harassment" frame presumed that Judge Thomas was guilty. But when Democrat Clinton was the target, scandal events are explained in terms of political combat. The subtext of this coverage is that the Democrat Clinton is innocent of any serious wrongdoing.

When Thomas was the target, the press went after the story like a pack of hungry wolves. The target was guilty and they were going to bring him to justice. But when Democratic President William Clinton was the target, the press showed little interest in the story.

When Thomas was the target, accuser Hill was treated as a brave heroine standing up for all decent women everywhere. But when Clinton was the target, the press sneeringly painted Paula Jones as a tramp who was a willing tool of Conservatives. On a Washington talk show, journalist Evan Thomas of *Newsweek* referred to her as "some sleazy woman with big hair coming out of the trailer parks." The press urged news consumers to believe that she was a low life.

Until November 1996, it looked as if this journalistic miscarriage were going fade into plausible deniability. However, there was an unexpected reversal of political fortune. By the fall of 1996, it became clear that the Paula Jones Harassment Case would end up in the Supreme Court. This meant that her case against the President of the United States was not as frivolous as the press had claimed, at least indirectly. It suddenly became possible for President Clinton to be sued in court for sexual harassment! If the President were convicted, the elite press would look like hypocritical partisan fools. Even if he were only convicted in the court of public opinion, Democrats and the press would still lose big time. Ironically, the same Judge Clarence Thomas whom Professor Anita Hill tried to bring down would sit in judgement on the Paula Jones Case.

After Democrat Clinton was safely elected President in November of 1996, some in the press began a public reappraisal of the Paula Jones case. Journalist Stuart Taylor wrote an article for the *American Lawyer* magazine. Basically he said that Jones actually had a case and that it was stronger than the case Professor Hill had against Judge Thomas. Responding to the Taylor article, journalist William Powers went on to analyze the early coverage of Paula Jones in a December 16, 1996, *New Republic* article. As the Paula Jones Case neared the Supreme Court, *Newsweek* revised its version of the story.

In January of 1997, journalist Evan Thomas went on a number of television shows to eat his unkind words about Ms. Jones. He even admitted to "partisan bias and cultural bias" and said that double standards in journalism should end. And in the January 13, 1997, issue of *Newsweek*, journalists Evan Thomas and Michael Isikoff put the confession in writing. While I commend *Newsweek* for going against the dominant Liberal culture and revising the story, I don't think it is too much to ask journalists to simply get the facts right the first time.

The Supreme Court decided that the Paula Jones case against President Clinton could go forward and need not wait till Clinton's term of office is over. Her case was subsequently thrown out of court by an Arkansas judge who ruled that even if everything she charged were true, it would not rise to the level of sexual harassment. This was, of course, a very Conservative idea of sexual harassment. But Jones accused Clinton of groping her. And Liberals in the press have been very quick to defend the decision putting those elite journalists in an interesting position of defending by default, a new "one-free-grope standard." Thus the press found Republican Thomas guilty of sexual harassment for allegedly talking dirty to a subordinate, while they found Clinton innocent of sexual harassment for allegedly groping an employee. This comparison provides clear evidence of the partisan double standard in the coverage of scandals.

SUMMARY

In authoritarian societies actual weapons are used to destroy people. In democracies we use virtual weapons, that is, information to destroy people. Scandals become the political weapon of choice. Partisans try to remove public servants from office, get people fired, and put "wrongdoers" in jail. Targets, of course, try to frustrate the designs of their accusers. The press is at the center of all scandals. The press is the mass medium through which scandal promoters and damage control teams must communicate to citizens. Journalists can make life easy or hard for scandal promoters and damage control teams, depending on whom they favor.

To this date, the press coverage of scandal events passes the test of political favoritism. Remember the idea of political favoritism is that one political party is treated very differently than another party. That is, *the liberal press constructs helpful scandal news for Democrats and disruptive scandal news for Republicans.* The coverage of scandals is shaped as much by the political prejudice of leading journalists as it is by any civic imperative to inform the public for the good of our democracy. If the press were fair, balanced and neutral, the traits of the coverage of scandal events would average the same for both Republicans and Democrats. But that is clearly not the case. The following traits of coverage provide a tangible measure of press favoritism.

1. <u>Attitude</u>. **When Democrats are the accusers, the Liberal press adopts the accuser attitude.** Republicans are presumed guilty. **When Republican are the accusers, the press adopts the target attitude.** Democrats are presumed innocent.

2. <u>Going After the Story</u>. **Energized by the prospect of bringing down a leading Republican, Liberal journalists pounce on the story. But when a Democrat is the target, a wave of apathy mysteriously sweeps through the ranks of the press.**

3. <u>Statute of Limitations</u>. **There is no statute of limitations for digging up dirt on Republicans, while journalists will find some statute of limitations for investigating targeted Democrats.**

4. <u>Standard of Conduct</u>. **The press holds Republicans to an unreasonably high standard of conduct.** Almost any charge against target

Republicans are judged to be serious. Almost any moral or ethical lapse may be enough to judge the offense serious. If a Republican tells a lie, it's a serious offense. Republicans are held responsible for the actions of all their associates.

However, the same **journalists hold Democrats to a very low standard.** Accusations against the target are usually judged to be frivolous. Lying does not even register on the scale journalists use to judge Democrats. When a close associate of a target Democratic is found guilty of a crime and sent to jail, journalists assess no responsibility to the target.

5. <u>Standard of Proof.</u> **It takes little actual evidence to judge a Republican target guilty.** The facts need only suggest Republican guilt. **However, there must be "hard solid proof" to judge a Democratic target guilty of anything.** When Democrats are the target, it takes a lot of evidence to prove guilt.

6. <u>Connecting the Dots.</u> **It's okay to go beyond the facts and tell the story, at least by suggestion, of Republican impropriety.** Journalists are quick to hype unproven stories of Republican wrongdoing. However, **it's bad journalism to *go beyond the facts* to even suggest that Democrats are guilty of any impropriety.** Journalists are quick to deflate any news of Democratic wrongdoing.

7. <u>Explaining Scandals.</u> **When Republicans are the target, scandal events are explained in terms of improper Republican behavior.** News products are peppered with attack questions and loaded scandal words. News stories are somber in tone. And the motives of the accusers are not important.

When Democrats are the target, scandal events are explained in terms of political combat as usual. Journalists are on their good verbal behavior. News stories now take on a sympathetic tone. The motives of Republican accusers are now very important. The target is given plenty of airtime to attack his Republican accusers.

8. <u>Scandal Impressions.</u> **When Republicans are the target, scandal stories give the impression that Republicans did something improper and unacceptable.** If journalists don't have any evidence of a scandal story, they can still suggest that a serious scandal looms in the near future.

(Coverage of the October Surprise provides a good example.) **When Democrats are the target, scandal stories give the impression Democrats are innocent of any serious wrongdoing and voters should approve of them.** Journalists often give the impression that the accusations are frivolous.

Some scandal coverage is more strikingly partisan than other coverage. Some scandal news displays most of the above traits. Other scandals news displays only some of these characteristics. However, there is enough partisan spin to have a powerful effect on public opinion.

DISCUSSION

When I studied the coverage of political scandals, the difference between the image of Republican scandals and Democratic scandals seen on the evening news was stunning. Thus, I sought to discover the nature of that press coverage. As I monitored the news of the scandals and attempted scandals of the last decade, a pattern of political speech emerged. All the targets seemed to have a similar attitude regardless of their political party. All accusers seemed to have a similar attitude regardless of political party. That political speech is summarized in the accuser and target attitude described above.

A consistent pattern of news coverage also emerged. The elite press consistently constructed the scandal news from the point of view of partisan Democrats. I studied the press coverage of many scandals and came up with the traits listed in the above summary. The traits go a long way to explain the sometimes stunningly different coverage of Republican and Democratic scandals.

Perception bias can explain much of the above double standard which characterizes the coverage of scandals and attempted scandals. Most journalists are Liberal Democrats and one would expect that the partisan perceptions of leading journalists play a role in news making. However, scandal attacks on the Republicans are so pointed and defense of Democrats so shameless, that perception bias becomes an inadequate explanation. A press actively engaged in the battle for public opinion on behalf of the Democrats provides a more comprehensive explanation of scandal coverage.

END NOTES

(1) This is *the muckraking tactic.* See, **The Muckrakers and American Society**, Edited by Herbert Shapiro, published by D.C. Heath and Company, Boston, in 1968 for a discussion on muckraking.

(2) It is often stated that the law was violated in the Iran/Contra Scandal, as if the alleged crime were legally obvious and a proven legal fact. Neither is true. Just because an act is signed by the president, it does not mean it is constitutional. Just because the President did not challenge the law in court, does not mean that it was legal. The subject of the legality of these amendments is up for dispute.

(3) For instance see page 733 of **The Oxford of History The American People**, written by Samuel Eliot Morrison, Published by Oxford University Press in New York in 1965. "The Democrats, determined to make reform the issue of the campaign, chose Governor Samuel J. Tilden, a wealthy but honest lawyer of Albany Regency background who had exposed the Tweed and similar political rings battening on the canal system of New York. Every paragraph of the Democratic platform began with 'Reform is necessary to win ...' and indeed it was. So much dirt was exposed in the campaign of 1876 that it seemed impossible for the Republicans to win again. But 'waving the bloody shirt' was still effective. 'Every man that shot at Union soldiers was a Democrat!' screamed Robert G. Ingersoll, ... 'The man that assassinated Lincoln was a Democrat. Soldiers, every scar you have got on your heroic bodies was given you by a Democrat!' ... "

Chapter 9

REINVENTING JOURNALISM

If truth is the first casualty of political warfare, it was probably gunned down by a corps of journalists with a social conscience. Thinking they are doing the people's work, the Liberal press brazenly meddles in elections and tries to influence public policy. When journalists orchestrate the shape and flow of the news in an effort to influence public opinion, the truth cannot survive. Yes, the Liberal press gets most of its "facts" mostly right, but the facts are embedded in an opinionated context which overwhelms the truth.

So, what is the truth anyway? I suggest that there are three kinds of truth. There is: (1) a truth we all use in our private lives, (2) a truth we must use as members of society, and (3) the real truth. If you were stranded on a tropical island with no other human being, you would not have to argue with anyone over what is true and what is not. You would determine for yourself what is true and simply act on it. You could live by your own truth. Of course, the real truth puts certain conditions on your private truth. You have to eat to live. Gravity keeps you firmly attached to the island. Day follows night in a regular pattern, etc.

But most of us live with other people. If we all lived only by our own private truth, the system would be called anarchy. To avoid such chaos, most of us opt for some system of order. People have devised various systems for agreeing on an official truth that all could use in their dealings with each other. A political system by which citizens help decide official truth is called democratic. A system by which one or a very few people decide on official truth is called authoritarian.

AUTHORITARIAN TRUTH

People tend to join political groups which share the same private truth. Bolstered by people who think just like they do, in-group members tend to think that their private truth is good for everybody everywhere. This group-centrism motivates some groups to try to impose their private truth on all of society. These groups think that ordinary citizens can't discover the truth on their own. These groups think that citizens need a powerful president or a ruling elite to discover the truth for them. These groups are authoritarian.

It is characteristic of the authoritarian style of thinking to see no difference between private truth and what should be the official truth shared by members of society. The authoritarian style of thinking is common. Even in democratic societies, the unspoken goal of most political groups is to win power and impose their version of the truth on everybody else. This makes sense to most political in-groups, because they see themselves as the sole possessors of the truth.

From the authoritarian perspective, the truth is something to be possessed. In the authoritarian view, the truth is possessed by the strong leader and/or an enlightened elite. In authoritarian societies, official truth is a body of politically correct "facts" discovered by the leader and his elite minions. This is important. Those authoritarian elites believe that they actually have easy access to "the truth." They believe that they have special powers of discerning the truth which out-groups and ordinary citizens don't have. Thus, authoritarians become intolerant of non-elites who claim to know "the facts."

In authoritarian societies, the press is a voice for disseminating official truth to ordinary citizens. Authoritarian news organizations present the image of current events forced through the same ideological prism they share with the leader. People with dissenting perceptions are not allowed access to mass media. The authoritarian news is not merely a matter of political correctness; the news is used to mobilize citizens to behave in the way the elite think best. Authoritarians see ordinary citizens as incapable of figuring out what is best for themselves.

The Liberal press is not authoritarian in the sense that it is an official organ of the central government. However, the Liberal news does display certain authoritarian traits. For instance, the elite press is a political monoculture. Nine out of ten working journalists are political Liberals who have little tolerance for political Conservatives. While it has lost some power to Rush Limbaugh, C-SPAN, Christian Broadcasting, Rupert Murdoch, computer networks and talk radio, the Liberal press still decides what will become news and how it will be presented. The Liberal press still acts as if it possesses official truth. In other words, nothing is true unless a small group of elite Liberal journalists says it's true.

Like the authoritarian news, the Liberal news is constructed to achieve definite political goals. Under the rubric of *social responsibility*, Liberal journalists take sides in political disputes. Journalists go to political disputes with the attitude that one side is "logically" right. Of course, it always turns out that the Liberal Democrats are "logically" right. Thus the press delivers a news which gives the Liberal political agenda a good hearing, while exhibiting hostility to competing agendas.

Like the authoritarian news, the Liberal news is based on the idea that ordinary citizens can't do for themselves. While journalists do favor democracy, they don't trust news consumers with raw news information. Leading journalists constantly claim that raw news information must be "filtered" before it gets to the public. Journalists think that news consumers will draw the wrong conclusions if journalists do not filter the raw news. As they see it, ordinary citizens don't have the intelligence to accomplish the task. As the Liberal press sees it, there are bad people out there, who will use information to cynically manipulate public opinion. Of course, those bad people are Republicans, businessmen, the military under Republican Presidents, and other Conservative types.

THE REAL TRUTH

Information is always a mess because it is: (1) often massive but incomplete, (2) usually confusing and contradictory, (3) always costly to gather, and (4) produced and consumed by people with flawed mental capabilities. Conclusions drawn from a body of information can be very sensitive to small changes in that information.

If you gather information about some event and pile it on your desk, you will soon discover that the information has certain characteristics. Some information seems sound or indisputable. Other information is good as far as it goes, but will have big gaps. There will be rumor and hearsay. Some information will be ambiguous. Other information will be outright contradictory. Some information is obviously false. All the information on your desk is produced by imperfect people who were confronted with a similar information problem. It soon becomes clear that the exact truth of the past event is not clear. It is often frustrating. It is also the natural state of affairs and has been referred to as the "bloomin', buzzin', confusion."[1] The difficulty of discovering the facts of any event is what might be called *the information problem*.

If you are ever asked to serve on a jury, do so. You may encounter the information problem as the jury tries to figure out if a crime occurred and who perpetrated it. You may hear conflicting expert testimony. The physical evidence may point to both guilt *and* innocence. You may hear witnesses to the same event tell very different stories. There may be some reason to believe that the defendant is innocent and there may be reason to believe he is guilty. Thus, the verdict will be an educated guess. Information often exhibits this annoying characteristic.

You could gather lots and lots of information about some event, yet the precise piece of data needed to draw any conclusion is not available. So the information available is usually incomplete. The incompleteness of information is important, because one single little new fact can change the whole picture deduced from analysis of the information. Thus, conclusions are very sensitive to small changes in any body of information.[2]

Information is never free. At some point somebody has to gather it, categorize it, evaluate it and integrate it into an information product like an academic paper, a newspaper, an encyclopedia, a television documentary or the evening news. This effort requires the expenditure of resources, energy and money to acquire and process the desired information. But resources, people, time and money are always limited. People must choose to gather this information and ignore that information. Consequently, information always has value.

Finally, we handle information with limited and flawed cognitive capabilities. Even if God were to gave us a complete body of absolutely true information and a table big enough to pile it on, we would not live long enough to consider all of it. And if God were to give us a life span long enough to examine the information, we would still have problems, because human perceptions and habits of thought are sloppy and error prone. Without such incredible help from God, we necessarily distort the evaluation of the information.

However, this situation does not mean that there is no real truth. Just because it is extremely difficult to discover the exact nature of some event, that does not mean that the event did not occur. Just because the nature of the physical universe is difficult to discover does not mean the physical universe does not exist. Just because information is a mess and people have flawed mental capacity does not mean that people can't discover anything.

How does one discover the truth from this "bloomin', buzzin' confusion" of information? I think that a reformulation of the question might help. Instead of asking, "How do *I* discover the truth," perhaps one should ask, "How do *we*, as a society, discover the truth?" For many years, people working in the law, science and other democratic institutions have been doing just that.

DEMOCRATIC TRUTH

As noted, in authoritarian societies, truth is something that citizens get from the government. In democratic societies, it's the other way around. In democratic societies, citizens have the primary role in setting official truth. Democratic institutions are built on the idea that the truth is exceedingly difficult to discover and that nobody has a monopoly on it. The democratic path to the truth recognizes that there is a "blooming, buzzing confusion" and implements some process designed to approach the truth. That is, democratic truth is a *process* in which (1) many people have an input, (2) in accordance with a set of rules and practices, (3) over a period of time.

Let's take another look at a courtroom. Judges and juries are faced with the daunting task of discovering the facts of some event in the past. There may be physical evidence such as fingerprints, DNA tests, hair, fibers, gum wrappers, tire treads and handwritten communications. Yet the evidence may not be conclusive. That's the usual situation. There may be conflicting testimony from experts. There may also be conflicting testimony from witnesses who have their own hidden agendas. The jury must sift through this evidence and reach a conclusion. Even after the jury has reached a verdict, the legal process is not necessarily over. There is a review process. The defendant can appeal to a higher court. Other judges may review court decisions. Verdicts may be affirmed or overturned.

Juries can reach the wrong verdict. Guilty people may go free. Innocent people may be jailed. But there is an important principle here. The legal process of discovering truth may not always be just, but it is the best path to justice. The democratic justice process is superior to the capricious justice one usually finds in authoritarian societies. Our highly flawed system of justice is far better than totalitarian justice which simply carts suspects off to a death camp.

The practice of science provides another example of democratic truth. The scientific method is a process designed to discover truth about the physical universe. For a hypothesis to become scientific fact, it must meet certain requirements. The hypothesis must be testable. Scientists must develop supporting evidence. Scientists must publish their findings. Other scientists must be able to review the evidence and repeat any supporting experiments.

In a way, democratic truth is all about developing processes for evaluating information which minimize the worst effects of cognitive biases and errors. Developing a process for the dissemination of news (information) to a mass audience should adhere to an ideal of democratic truth.

JOURNALISTIC TRUTH

Compared to the other more rigorous methodologies for seeking democratic truth, the practice of discovering journalistic truth is in a primitive stage of development. Lacking discipline and professional standards, journalists freely abuse their position of power. Armed with their social conscience, journalists charge into the politics of winning the hearts and minds of the public to various "good" (Liberal) causes. This social conscience may have begun high-mindedly, but becomes partisan by the time it gets to the front page. The theory of social responsibility suggests that journalists "afflict the comfortable and comfort the afflicted." In practice journalists afflict Republicans and comfort Democrats. Misleading news consumers in the service of a higher social good becomes respectable journalism.

This sort of activist truth-seeking leads to the neo-authoritarian news described above. In my opinion, the press establishment should change directions and move toward a more democratic news. This will not be easy. Journalists will need to change their way of thinking about the truth. They should move away from the idea that news is what a few elite journalists say it is, and the truth is a *thing* journalists possess. They should move towards the view that news is what citizens say it is, and truth is a *process* in which both journalists and citizens participate.

NEWS AS A QUALITY PROCESS

Like the other democratic methodologies of discovering truth, the news should be thought of as much a process as a product. For this to happen, the news needs to be reinvented from the ground up. The culture of the press establishment needs to undergo radical change. The following is intended as a possible starting point for a new discussion of quality news.

The United States Constitution establishes the idea that a free press is a necessary requirement for a democracy. The idea is that informed citizens are free citizens. It was thought that a free wheeling press would eventually produce enough truth to run a democracy. Thus, journalists were left totally free to define news. Journalists are also free to abuse press freedom. They can define the news to fit their private political prejudices. While such a practice of journalism is an obnoxious abuse of power, legal constraints on press freedom will create a worse result. I agree with this idea of press freedom. Within the incredibly loose bounds of libel law, journalists should be free to air whatever they desire.

At the present time, journalists are very good at providing the information required by Liberal Democrats to make informed decisions. In my opinion, journalists have responsibility to provide the same information service to the other major political constituencies. Journalists might begin to think about what it means to deliver quality news to a politically diverse society.

This idea of press responsibility suggests a definition of news. News might be defined as information about important current events that people would demand if they knew it were available. In order to do that, it seems reasonable that **journalists should become facilitators of a news process which delivers enough reliable information about important current events to a pluralistic public in time for them to make informed**

decisions. This would require profound changes in the way the news business is conducted.

Pluralistic

Journalists should actually become honest brokers of information to a diverse society.³ Journalists should become sensitive to the fact that the majority of news consumers are not political Liberals. Journalists could encourage feedback from news consumers. Perhaps leading journalists could staff the public relations phones one day a month. Perhaps that exposure would raise the consciousness of journalists. In any case, there needs to be a process for serious consideration of feedback from news consumers.

After learning that most citizens are not political Liberals, journalists really need to learn to acknowledge the legitimacy of non-Liberal points of view. At the present time, the press doesn't. Interviews with Conservative Republicans are a contact sport for most elite journalists. Republican bashing has nothing to do with gathering the news. Journalists can be civil and still gather the news. Civility is an indication of political tolerance. Civility should be a characteristic of professional journalism.

A new, more tolerant press would include politically diverse points of view into the process of making news. As of June, 1998, newsrooms don't look like America. Studies suggest that newsrooms look like the Liberal wing of the Democratic party. Press organizations could employ affirmative action for non-Liberals. In order to look like America, big league newsrooms should be staffed with Republicans, Democrats, Conservatives, Liberals, Libertarians and Populists.⁴ Racial affirmative action has created racially diverse public institutions. Perhaps political affirmative action could create politically diverse newsrooms.

Timely

Information of current events is not news unless it gets to citizens in a timely fashion! News of current events should get to all major news-consuming constituencies in time for them to make informed decisions and take any appropriate action. Journalists should not sit on a news story (till it becomes harmless) just because it might hurt a favored Liberal politician. Journalists should not rush a story into print, just because it might hurt a hated politician. News should flow to the public in a natural fashion, unencumbered by partisan passions. Conservatives, Libertarians and Populists also deserve to have the news they need in time to make decisions and use in political process.

Reliable

It seems fundamental that the news should have a reasonable level of reliability. If news is not reliable, it is of little use to citizens. I take reliable to mean that a news story is as truthful as possible, given press deadlines. But what does that mean? If journalistic facts were the result of the scientific process, it would take years to get any news. So, a journalistic fact is a much squashier thing requiring a lower standard of proof.

However, there must be a higher standard than the word of a journalist. It's not good enough for journalists to merely assert that, "It's true because I say it's true." A democratic process for determining journalistic truth needs more than the authority of a leading journalist. Too often that authority is based on partisan perceptions. Journalistic facts must meet certain minimum requirements. To begin with, it must be possible, in a practical sense, to verify a journalistic fact.

Let me illustrate the difference between a fact that can be verified and a partisan perception. A journalist might make the statement, "It is a fact Pat Buchanan entered the New Hampshire primary in a bid for the 1992 Republican nomination for President." I could verify the Buchanan candidacy by going to New Hampshire and checking with the local election bureaucracy. I could check newspaper coverage of the election. If I don't have the time or money to do all that, I am forced to rely on some other observer such as a news magazine.

But what about the following statement from *Newsweek* of January 1992, "The paranoid style in American politics fits Patrick J. Buchanan like a comfortable old coat of iron mail." Is that statement a fact? Is "the paranoid style in American politics" a fact? What is "the paranoid style in American politics" anyway? The Liberals at *Newsweek* think they know. But what verification procedure did they use? Did they convene a panel of politically neutral psychiatrists to interview Mr. Buchanan and render a diagnosis of his psycho-political mental state? More likely, the above characterization of Mr. Buchanan is a Liberal prejudice common in the elite media.

It is a fact that Pat Buchanan ran for President. He may actually be paranoid. He may be sane and fond of "the paranoid style of politics." However, *Newsweek* neither presented nor referred to evidence to support this partisan accusation. Making such declarations without reference to supporting evidence is the authoritarian style of journalism. This partisan brew of fact and fiction too often passes for actual news. Such news is not reliable.

The press should at least reduce the worst effects of their political prejudices. They could get back to the old-fashioned idea of "just the facts ma'am." When providing information about an important current event, journalists should tell news consumers "who, what, where and when." These basic facts can be verified by independent observers. Journalists should leave the "why" of any event to the editorial page. The "why" of important complex events can be highly subjective and argued about for decades. Quality news is based on a core of hard facts and a minimum of journalist opinion.

Quality journalistic facts have supporting evidence. Quality news stories have at least two sources. There needs to be at least two adults who will testify to the truth of the story. There should be some sort of physical evidence, even if it is circumstantial. I refer here to documents, letters, video, transcripts, etc. And the press should make this supporting evidence available to the public.

Representative

Many journalists claim to merely hold up a mirror to the world. However, the image in the mirror is the inside of the newsroom rather than the real world outside. For instance, the selection of guests on talk news programs does not represent the diversity of opinion from the political process. Consider the CNN talk news show, *CNN & Company*. Participants in this half-hour program discuss the hot issues of the day. A Liberal-leaning CNN journalist moderates a discussion with three other persons. There is usually a Republican or Conservative, a Democrat or a Liberal, and another Liberal journalist from some other news organization.

The two journalists typically side with the Democrat/Liberal guest making it three against the one Republican/Conservative.

The notion of representativeness comes from the subject of statistics, and journalists should adapt the idea to their work. The subject of statistics is all about discovering the characteristics of a population of things (or people) using samples from that population. Consider how pollsters discover public opinion. It is not possible to ask every adult American any question. So pollsters telephone only a small sample of people. They work hard to make sure that sample is representative of the American population. If done correctly, the characteristics of the sample will be close to actual characteristics of the population of American citizens. Journalists could begin a process which leads to a news that is more representative of reality.

Constantly Correct The Record

After journalists present their version of some event, there is a tendency to stand by that story as if absolute proven fact. The statement, "We stand by our story," should be banned from the journalistic lexicon. Too often it's just an excuse for bad journalism. Even when there is substantial evidence that a news story is wrong, few news organizations make a serious attempt to make the correction. Journalists typically let the false image remain.

Journalists ought to take the process of correcting and updating past stories seriously. Review of important news stories should be a regular activity. I don't mean the kind of self-serving review conducted by the public relations designed to increase audience share. I do mean that journalists should review news stories with the attitude that the truth is a process. When new information comes in, stories should be reviewed with an eye to the possibility that something entirely different may have happened. And when that happens, journalists should report the revised story as news.

Make Consistent News Judgements

At present, there is a double standard in news judgements. When covering leading Republicans, the Liberal press provides a tenaciously aggressive counterpoint. They claim that it is their "watchdog role." When covering leading Democrats, the press looks more like a lapdog. This behavior is one more example the partisan nature of the elite press. It is typical of partisans to use one standard for judging their in-group fellows and apply another standard to enemy out-groups.

For the news to be pluralistic there needs to be one standard of proof for all. There can't be one standard for friends and another for enemies. There can't be one standard for Conservative Republicans and another for Liberal Democrats. For instance, there is a double standard for judging the veracity of news sources. The studies by Dr. Robert Lichter show that the press considers Liberal news sources much more reliable than Conservative sources.

Journalists also employ a partisan double standard for judging the facts of events. Consider scandal events for instance. When covering scandal events, the Liberal press requires "hard solid proof" to declare a Democrat guilty. On the other hand elite journalists are quite happy to suggest Republican guilt based on the slightest shred of evidence. See the previous chapter for a discussion of the shifting standards.

The press should be consistent. If journalists are going to provide a counterpoint to the Republicans, they should treat the Democrats the same way. The Liberal press should learn how to treat all political participants alike. Journalists should give Conservative, Populist and Libertarian ideas the same good hearing that they give to Liberal ideas. Journalists need to learn how to be tolerant of people and ideas they don't like. It should be a quality news goal to actually promote a marketplace of ideas.

SELF-POLICING

Unless journalists break a law, they are not accountable to the American people for anything they do. They can't be defeated at elections. They can't be recalled. They are not subject to petition. They can tell big lies to achieve vulgar partisan ends and get away with it. If you complain about press excesses, journalists will say that they don't have to be held to a high standard because they are not elected to office.

I dispute that bold assertion. (1) While not elected to public office, journalists act and talk as if they were a kind of semi-official agency commissioned to supply the authentic version of events to American citizens. (2) As self-appointed guardians of truth, journalists should have high standards of conduct. (3) High standards are required to maintain public trust in news information disseminated by the press.

So what should happen when journalists allow partisan favoritism to distort the news or when they mislead the public or violate standards of conduct or otherwise behave badly? As much as I would like it to be otherwise, the press should police itself. Any effort to impose high standards on the press from outside will only make matters worse. Self-policing is the only way to improve the quality of the news.

Journalists could begin the process by ending their **code of silence**. Journalists get very moralistic about the police, the military and other professions, when those organizations protect the wrongdoers in their own ranks from criticism. However, journalists have their own code of silence. Elite journalists will rarely rat on a colleague. Even so-called media critics rarely level serious criticism at other journalists.

One thing that individual journalists are particularly silent about is their own political leanings. That should end. I think there should be **truth in information packaging**. As we saw by the examination of perception bias, the political leanings of journalists can influence on how the news is gathered, produced and presented. When journalists have an interest in the outcome of political contests, they are surely tempted to stack the coverage to help favored politicians and causes. That's why the people have **a right to know** the political leanings of the journalists who supply the news which lubricates our democracy.

Journalists should also tell news consumers more about their news sources. If journalists are going to uncritically use press releases from activist groups like the Environmental Defense Fund as a source of unchallenged truth, people have a right to know the political leanings of these partisan groups. Journalists should routinely present enough information about news sources for citizens to determine the partisan motivations of the source.

Organizations like Common Cause and the Children's Defense Fund support Liberal causes and work against Conservative causes. They wear the "non-partisan" label only by the mechanism of a legal fiction. In the narrow legal eyes of federal agencies, a political group is "non-partisan" if it does not specifically tell people to vote for or against any particular candidate. Thus, activist groups participate in elections under the rubric of providing "educational" information to the public.

In other words, there should be truth in packaging for news sources as well as journalists. That's why journalists should never use anonymous sources. Truth in packaging is hostile to the idea that a source should be anonymous. The information distortion caused by unnamed sources far outweighs any information benefits to citizens. The temptation to abuse press power is just too great. Too often journalists use anonymous sources to make personal attacks on politicians they don't like. Anonymous sources are too often a way of disguising editorial opinion.

Indirect speech is another way of editorializing the news. Journalists apparently think they can express their opinion in news stories as long as they do it indirectly "between the lines." The practice of using indirect speech to editorialize the news should just stop. It's not complicated. News belongs on the front page. Editorials belong on the opinion page. Editorials do not belong in the middle of a hard news story even if stated in an indirect, implied manner.

CITIZEN JOURNALISM

I think the chances of reforming the likes of Dan Rather and Peter Jennings are nil. As with the rest of the elite press corps, they are powerful people accustomed to employing the evening news in the service of *good* causes. They are proud of their efforts to induce America to adopt the Liberal agenda as fundamental social policy. Their words suggest that they see themselves fending off mean Conservatives who would ravage the working class for selfish gain. The press culture is infused with this ultimately very partisan notion called social responsibility. It is not likely that the press establishment will relinquish its position of power and produce a neutral objective news or even move in that direction.

I do not favor government intervention to correct press abuses. I am even skeptical about private news councils. These types of measures lead to a politically correct news that is much worse than the abuse of press power we presently experience. If the organized press refuses to reform, then private citizens should get involved. This is a free country. Freedom of the press belongs to everyone, not just those "those who own a press." Until now, only a privileged few people had access to a mass audience.

But times are changing. The Internet has made it possible for any citizen to gain access to a mass audience. The old notion that only journalists can land the same message on every doorstep, is no longer true. Citizens with only modest incomes can post "news" on the internet. Each of the millions of web sites is exposed to the whole world. It is now possible for any citizen to become a journalist, a "citizen journalist."

Maybe an "ordinary" citizen can't break the big story; however, most people could do the job that most journalists actually do. A citizen does not have to be at the scene of breaking events to get the story and give it a new angle. In fact, a lot of journalism is done over the phone. And journalism is not rocket science. Anyone with an average IQ can learn how to do it. It's a matter of learning how to be an observer. Learning how to set aside biases is of course difficult. However, I suspect that an ordinary citizen can do at least as good a job as our leading journalists. At the very least, citizen journalists can add a little pluralism to the news business. Journalism is too important to be left to journalists. News is everybody's business.

POSTSCRIPT

I was a software engineer before I began my study of the news. On some software development projects I worked in software quality assurance. I reviewed the work of development engineers and made recommendations for improvement. Time was always limited. I soon learned to concentrate only on the serious problems and ignore the nit-picking stuff. My goal was to make recommendations designed to improve the quality of the software. I intend to do the same for the process of developing news.

As I began to understand media bias, I soon realized that fundamental change was required. Political prejudice, partisan bias and ideological bias are pervasive. These biases are entrenched in the very culture of the elite press. As my study continued, I realized that an authoritarian view of the truth was integral to the prejudiced style of thinking. Other professions tended to view the truth as a process, while journalists continue to view the truth as a possession. It was clear that journalism has to be reinvented.

It is not possible to eradicate all media bias from the press. It is not even possible to fully describe how that might be done. That would require god-like knowledge. However, as is done with the development of software, journalists can squeeze out the worst biases and errors. This task does not require god-like knowledge of the truth or herculean efforts by mortal journalists. As journalists constantly strive to improve the quality of news products, they can identify the worst press practices and eliminate them. Over time, I think the press could learn how to deliver quality information about current events to a politically diverse public.

END NOTES

(1) For reference to the expression "bloomin', buzzin', confusion" see page 462 of *The Principles of Psychology* by William James, originally published in 1890, the 1983 edition published by Harvard University Press in Cambridge, MA.

(2) Edison's light bulb is a good example. He expended a of lot effort testing various filaments. But just one word, *tungsten*, made the difference between dark and light for millions of people.

(3) This expression has been attributed to Anchorperson Dan Rather of CBS.

(4) See the book, **Beyond Liberal and Conservative** by William S. Maddox and Stuart A. Lilie, published by the Cato Institute in 1984. The Cato Institute promotes a Libertarian point of view. The authors do a comprehensive review of data that indicates the ideological segmentation of American citizens. They found four large ideological constituencies: Conservative, Liberal, Populist and Libertarian.

APPENDIX A

GLOSSARY

This glossary contains definitions of some words used in this book. The words defined here are from basically three origins: (1) Dictionary usage, (2) Popular slang, and (3) Words the author modified to fit a special vocabulary need. This latter usage was kept to a minimum.

activist. Webster defines activism as "a doctrine or practice that emphasizes direct vigorous action (as a mass demonstration) in support of or opposition to one side of a controversial issue." What characterizes an activist is that judgements of fact are not made on the basis of merit, logic or reason, but instead on the politics of advancing *the cause*. Activists tend to think that the righteousness of their cause supersedes the truth. Civility and tolerance are seen as weakness. In short, activists are at war.

activist journalist. Apparently many journalists see their unique position as an opportunity to advance "good" causes. Consciously or unconsciously, they are willing to make news judgements that help the good cause. Of course, those causes are always of the Liberal variety. The use of the news to further causes is not journalism in a pluralistic society.

activist group. This is a organization which uses certain well-known public relations techniques to get free political advertising in the news. Many activists are media wise and know how to use television to create events which further their cause. When a big corporation uses public relations to get its commercial messages into the news free of charge, it is called a media event by reporters. When Liberal activist political groups do the same thing to get their political messages into the news free of charge, it is called "news" by a sympathetic media elite.

angle. An angle is "an approach to a story." [adapted from Hohenberg, 1983]

attack journalism. This form of reporting the news is more than simple negative press; it is designed to hurt political enemies. An attack story may be quite true. But the reason it is becomes news is its political value, not its news value.

back-paging. This expression refers to the practice of partisan newspapers which puts news that hurts political friends on the back pages of their newspaper. On the television news, it is the practice of downplaying news which hurts political friends.

bias. From Webster's, bias is, "an inclination of temperament or outlook." As used here, bias means "prejudice." However, the word bias, as used by some journalists and professional observers of the media, "bias" is coming to mean "a conscious intent to slant the news."

broad brushing. This is the verbal use of "guilt by association" to taint a whole group because the alleged sins of a few.

center of the news. Stories that appear on the front page or one of the three lead stories on the evening news are at the center of the news. Besides being "front paged," stories in the center of the news tend to be consistent with each other. There is a consistent set of presuppositions in the center of the news. The center of the news tends to reflect a single worldview. A story suggesting a non-Liberal point of view may appear on the front page. But then it will be ignored as if it never occurred. I don't consider such stories to be at the center of the news.

characterization. A characterization is a shorthand definition, a description or caricature of a thing, a person or an event. A characterization is a usually verbal picture of how a person "reads" a situation or a person or a process etc. Everybody does not characterize events in the same way. The way an event is characterized indicates how that person looks at the world.

cognition. This is the mental process by which knowledge is acquired. Cognition includes perception, recall from memory, and other thinking tasks. For more discussion on this see page 167 of *Social Psychology & Modern Life*, second edition, consulting editor, Philip G. Zimbardo, Alfred A. Knopf, New York, 1980, or some other similar text.

copy. Material written by a journalists is known as copy.

correspondent. In print journalism the term has been used to describe a reporter who is not in town, like a foreign correspondent or a war correspondent. In broadcast journalism it is a job classification above the basic newsperson. [adapted from Hohenberg, 1983]

crusade. A crusade is an effort by all parts of the editorial staff to persuade the public to do something perceived to be in the public interest by the news organization. [Hohenberg, 1983] Thus, a crusading journalist would appear to be an activist journalist.

editorial. "Comment on the news in the name of the news organization itself." [Hohenberg, 1983]

handlers. These are advisors who help political candidates create a good media image. A "handler" in this context is a public relations professional who helps a candidate for public office with their media image. The term is often used against Republican candidates for public office by political commentators who favor the Democratic candidate. This makes a kind of partisan sense. Democratic partisans, no doubt, "see" Republican presidential victories as a crass manipulation of public opinion rather than a winner of a fair fight. The use of the word handler in this context subtly communicates the idea that Republican politicians have no values. They need handlers to win. The idea is that Republicans merely say what their handlers tell them to say in order to get elected. Democrats don't have handlers; they have advisors. When it is obvious that the Democrats won because they were "handled," the press admires their adroit political ability.

hidden in plain sight. This is the art of presenting news, while at the same time discouraging public interest in the same news. It can be relegated to the margins. For instance, the draft record of Democratic President William Clinton is still hidden in plain sight. Presenting facts in an unconnected fashion is also a way to hide information in plain sight. This leaves only the aggressive news consumer to "connect the dots."

hyping a story. This is the practice of making a story more important than its intrinsic news value. Hyping gives artificial legs to a story, even when there is no new information. Old news is repackaged to keep public attention focused upon it.

ideology. The word "ideology" comes from the word idea. My dictionary says that ideology refers to a "systematic body of concepts," "the thinking characteristic of an individual or group." Thus, a political ideology is a systematic body of political concepts. The nuance of the meaning is that the ideas are integrated into a thoughtful whole. Partisans often use the word "ideology" as an epithet. As an accusation, an ideology is a simplistic body of stupid ideas ineptly applied by ideologues to solve problems they know nothing about.

intellectuals. These are people whose position in the world is derived from ideas.

loaded question. This is a question which is really an attack. A loaded question is packed with one-sided or prejudicial influences. A loaded question is a way of making an accusation without quite appearing to do so. A loaded question is a statement, not a question.

the margins of the news. Any published information that is not in the center of the news is at the margins. The margin of the news is the back pages or what amounts to the back pages in television news. The Conservative press is relegated to the margins of the news.

McCarthyism. McCarthyism is just a form of scandalmongering. It is characterized by personal attacks on those deemed subversive to the good of society. As is typical of much scandalmongering, accusers employ widely publicized, indiscriminate and unsubstantiated allegations to bring down their opponents. The word grew out of the Cold War. Senator Joseph McCarthy held a series of hearings in the early 1950s to investigate Communist influence in the government. Most Liberals saw little danger from the Communists. Thus, Liberals viewed Senator McCarthy as an intolerant bad guy who wrongly labeled Communists as subversive and sought to destroy them.

muckraking. This is the journalistic practice of seeking out information which will do harm to some public figure. Journalists claim to be merely exposing wrongdoing. Muckraking is a scandalmongering activity, thus the wrongdoing may be real or imagined. The term dates back to the progressive era at the turn of the century.

news analysis. News analysis is an editorial which is constructed to look and sound like a news report.

news. I define news as a representation of events which are vivid, close in distance, novel and have influence on news consumers. News is also information about important current events required by a politically diverse society to make informed decisions. Such events and information have news value. Other theories of news, like "social responsibility journalism," have different definitions of news value.

The New Deal. This is the name that Democrats gave to the socialist-style programs promoted by President Franklin Roosevelt in the 1930s. Many "New Deal" programs were first proposed by people who identified themselves as socialists. A "new deal" has the connotation of "freshness and equality of opportunity afforded by a fresh deal in a card game."

opinion. Unproven information held to be true. Not substantially different than the most general definition of prejudice. In journalism there is supposed to be a fire wall between hard news and editorial opinion.

piece A news story.

pool. One or more journalists who gather news for a larger group of journalists [adapted from Hohenberg 1983]. When covering combat, a pool is sometimes used. In that case a few reporters will cover the combat for all other reporters or correspondents.

ringer. Webster's defines a ringer as "one that enters a competition under false representations." It is this shade of meaning of ringer which I wish to draw upon and apply to the news business. For instance, a ringer could be an expert who has a political ax to grind, but is presented to news consumers as unbiased.

Scandalmongering. This is the practice of alleging improper behavior, real or imagined, with the intent to damage political opponents. The press is a key player because they communicate the allegations to a mass audience.

sitting on a story. When a news organization refuses to share information with the public that has news value, it is called sitting on a story. Journalists usually sit on stories that hurt political friends or help political enemies. Usually the story is aired at some later time.

softball questions. These are friendly easy questions usually asked of favored politicians to make them look good.

special interest group. This is a pejorative term referring to an enemy activist group.

spin. Spin is the presentation of information designed to influence public opinion. Spin is a word used mainly in connection with the electronic media. It can have both the verbal and visual aspects of bias. In addition it has the connotation of modem methods of persuasion directed by a hidden agenda. It is the belief of the author that the word "spin" is taken from the game of pool used as a model for language behavior. A player can put a "spin" on the cue ball thereby imparting a spin to another ball which would not otherwise have it. Using this model the following definition is drawn: Spin on a story is the impression given to the viewer, which is not justified by the facts presented.

stooge expert. This is a favored expert on an important subject who can be counted upon to support the beliefs of a journalist.

sweetheart interview. These are friendly little chats between a journalist and a newsmaker, passed off to news consumers as an interview.

unsupported predicate. This is a form of begging the question. A predicate is "something that is affirmed or denied of the subject in a proposition in logic (in "paper is white," whiteness is the predicate). Statements and questions have predicates. Part of the context of a statement is the unarticulated statements associated with the spoken or written statement. The lawyer's question, "When did you stop beating your wife?" has a predicate that the person being asked is a married man and that he beat his wife and at some point stopped. An unsupported predicate would be a predicate of a statement or question which is not supported by the facts presented in a story or reasonably available in the public domain. Spin usually has an unsupported predicate designed to influence public opinion.

worldview. This word will be used exactly as defined in the dictionary. From Webster's, "weltanschauung" which means "a comprehensive conception or apprehension of the world esp. from a specific standpoint."

xenophobic. The word in its general form refers to fear of and hostility for a person, an idea or anything which appears foreign. It comes from the Greek *xenos* (stranger) and *phobos* (fear). As I use it in this book, it most often refers to fear and hostility, which is political in nature, that is *political xenophobia*. This would be fear of political ideas not one's own.

zingers. According to Webster a zinger is "1: a pointed witty remark or retort 2: something causing or meant to cause interest, surprise, or shock." In the news a zinger is a non sequitur "wisecrack" stuck on the end of a television news story.

SOURCES FOR THE GLOSSARY

[Hohenberg 1983] John Hohenberg. **The Professional Journalist** by John Hohenberg published in San Francisco by Holt, Rinehart and Winston in 1983.

[Webster's dictionary]

APPENDIX B

IDEOLOGY

While there are some non-Liberal commentators, pundits and editorial writers in the press establishment, there are few non-Liberal voices in the reporting press. Newsrooms don't look like America. They look like the Liberal wing of the Democratic party. For every conservative Pat Buchanan or John MacLaughlin, there are many Liberal commentators. There are even fewer non-Liberal voices in the newsrooms of the elite press. With non-Liberal views all but locked out of many newsroom, conservatives have found a voice in what might be call the "alternate media." I am referring to radio talk shows, a few news shows on the networks and the religious channels on cable television.

Liberals dominate media way out of proportion to their constituent numbers in the general population. If one were to use the evening news to estimate the number of Liberals in the country, one would conclude that they made up 85 percent of the population. In fact, Liberals comprise about 20 percent of the population. There are other legitimate points of view. There are other political camps in the country beside the Liberals who have been around for some time.

It is worth noting that all the dominant political camps in America have their roots in the American liberalism (small "l") of the 19th century. This nineteenth century liberalism provides the intellectual framework of what we know as democratic values. These are ideas like individual rights, liberty and freedom. Different people have put different interpretations on these democratic values. The interpretations tend to fall into various political camps--Liberals, Conservatives, Libertarians and Populists. Each grouping has a different perception of individual rights, liberties, freedoms. All agree that individual rights, personal liberty and freedom are a good thing. The differences between the major political camps revolve around various interpretations and implementations of these agreed-upon democratic values. All political camps perceive themselves as the true inheritors of the democratic tradition, the real do-gooders, the true good guys, the proper representatives of the people.

LIBERTARIAN

Libertarians are not Liberals. In fact they are quite the opposite. The name "libertarian" comes from the word "liberty" rather than the word "liberal." Libertarians are the closest of all four major political camps to the 19th century of ideal of democratic liberalism (small "l" liberalism, that is).

Libertarians see government as a necessary evil. From this point of view, the primary job of government is to keep the public safety. Libertarians interpret that very narrowly. Libertarians tend to think that the Liberal welfare state benefits mostly bureaucrats rather than "the people" and would dismantle it. Libertarians favor most individual rights promoted by both Liberals and Conservatives. Libertarians believe in a free market with only the bare minimum of governmental policing. Libertarians give a strong meaning to the concepts of freedom and liberty. Libertarians interpret freedom to mean freedom to act rather than freedom from the nasty effects of things. Libertarians believe that freedom and responsibility are two edges of the same sword.

CONSERVATIVE

Conservatives and Libertarians have much in common. There are also important differences. Conservatives tend to favor a much smaller government than do Liberals, though not as small as Libertarians. Conservatives see the primary function of government as protecting citizens from crime and foreign invaders. Only when this has been done can the government turn its attention to other items.

While Conservatives tend to favor a more limited government than Liberals, they also are willing to use the power of the government to enforce their vision of a moral society. Unlike Liberals and Libertarians, Conservatives seek to control things like pornography, sexual behavior, gambling and other so-called vices.

Conservatives also believe in "individual rights," but they focus on a different set of rights than do Liberals. Conservatives see the "right to life" as the first civil right and the first duty of the government. Conservatives see the right to life and property as fundamental. Conservatives are interested in rights that protect individuals from excesses of government.

When Conservatives use the word freedom, they are talking about freedom to do things. Freedom to own private property, freedom to start a business, freedom to defend oneself from criminals and thugs, freedom to travel, etc. Conservatives are supporters of the free enterprise system but do favor more regulation than Libertarians. They see freedom as intrinsically linked to property rights.

POPULIST

Populists are always the loose cannons of the American political terrain. A goodly portion of the electorate falls into this category. Populists are reform-minded people who have been outraged by the behavior of government. Populists tend to make *popular* appeals intended to "to set the country right." Populist politicians from Governor Huey Long in the 1930s to Ross Perot in the 1990s have appealed to independent voters with this type of message. Populists come up with slogans like, "Let's clean up the mess in Washington."

INDIVIDUAL RIGHTS

Everyone favors individual rights. However, each of the primary political groupings has a somewhat different set of individual rights they consider important. There is general consensus on the individual rights that come under the heading of civil rights.

Liberals and Libertarians perceive an absolute right to privacy under which a woman has an unlimited right to abortion. Conservatives do not.

Conservatives, Libertarians, and many African-American Liberals perceive a fundamental individual right to keep and bear arms for the purpose of self-protection. Most Liberals do not support the right to keep and bear arms as an individual right. Liberals see the possession of firearms as a privilege that can be removed by simple legislation.

Liberals perceive a weak right to private property. Liberals tend to perceive the wealth of the country as property of the welfare state to use as it deems necessary. So there is a tendency of Liberals to consider the state and the planet as more important than individual property rights.

Conservatives and especially Libertarians perceive a very strong right to private property.

APPENDIX C

ANNOTATED BIBLIOGRAPHY

Included in this list are books which criticize the press from both the Liberal and Conservative point of view. Also included are books which one ought to be familiar with to be literate on the subject of news criticism.

Adler, Renata. *Reckless Disregard*. New York: Alfred A. Knopf, Inc., 1986.

Altheide, Arthur J. *Creating Reality: How the TV News Distorts Events*. Beverley Hills: Sage Publications, 1976. This book is a good readable criticism of the press from the radical Liberal point of view.

Braestrup, Peter. *Big Story*. Abridged Edition. New Haven: Yale University Press, 1978. This mammoth work is must reading for details about the how the press misreported the Tet Offensive during the Vietnam War in 1968. Although Mr. Braestrup tries to soften the blow to his fellow journalists, his book is worth reading for the abundant examples of an excessive lapse of professionalism on the part of Vietnam journalists.

Boorstin, Daniel. *The Image: A Guide to Pseudo-Events in America*. New York: Harper & Row 1961.

Chafets, Ze'ev. *Double Vision*. New York: William Morrow and Company Inc. 1985.

Cornwall Elmer E. *Presidential Leadership of Public Opinion* Bloomington: Indiana University Press. 1965. Especially see the table on page 235, for evidence that press releases were taken as released and printed during the Roosevelt and Kennedy administrations.

Cromer, Gerald, Character Assassination in the Press. In Charles Winick, ed., *Deviance and Mass Media*, pp. 225-241. Beverly Hills: Sage, 1978.

Efron, Edith. *The News Twisters*. Los Angles: Nash Publishing, 1971. This is the book that stirred up all the whole business of TV news bias.

Efron, Edith. *How CBS Tried to Kill a Book*. Los Angles: Nash Publishing, 1972. The book CBS allegedly tried to kill was *The News Twisters*.

Elgin, Suzette Haden. *More on the Gentle Art of Verbal Self-Defense*. Englewood Cliffs, New Jersey: Prentice-Hall, 1983. This is good to read because it discusses the notion that there are two meanings in our speech, that which comes from the direct meaning of what we say and that which is implied by what we say and how we say it.

Fry, Don. *Believing the News*. Institute for Media Studies, 1985.
A gathering of elite press journalists tells us that the press is quite credible.

Goldstein, Tom. *The News at Any Cost: How Journalists compromise their ethics to shape the news*. Simon and Schuster, 1985.

Graber, Doris A. *Mass Media and American Politics*. Washington D.C.: Congressional Quarterly Press, 1980.

Graham, Tim. *Pattern of Deception: The Media's Role in the Clinton Presidency*. Published by the Media Research Center: Alexandria, Virginia, 1996.

Hulteng, John L. *The Messenger's Motives: Ethical Problems of the News Media*. Englewood Cliffs, New Jersey: Prentice-Hall, 1985.

Iyengar, Shanto. *Is Anyone Responsible? How Television Frames Political Issues*. University of Chicago Press: Chicago, 1991. Good discussion on how contextual cues and hints can influence public opinion.

Iyengar, Shanto and Donald R. Kinder. *News That Matters*. University of Chicago Press: Chicago, 1987. Discussion on how agenda setting and priming influence public opinion.

Karetzky, Stephen and Goldman, Peter E. editors. *The Media's War Against Israel*. New York: Steimatzky Books, 1986.

Klaidman, Stephen and Tom L. Beauchamp. *The Virtuous Journalist*. New York and Oxford: Oxford University Press, 1987. Stephen Klaidman is a Senior Research Fellow at the Kennedy Institute of Ethics, Georgetown

University, and has been a journalist for the *International Herald Tribune*, the *Washington Post* and the *New York Times*. Tom L. Beauchamp is Professor of Philosophy and Senior Research Scholar at the Kennedy Institute and author or co-author of such books as *Principles of Biomedical Ethics*, *Philosophical Ethics*, and *Hume and the Problem of Causation*.

Lemert, James B. **Does Mass Communication Change Public Opinion After All?** Published by Nelson-Hall Chicago

Lichter, S. Robert, and others, ***Nuclear News*** Washington D.C.: Center for Media and Public Affairs, May 1986.

Lichter, S. Robert, and others. ***The Media Elite***. Bethesda, Maryland: Adler & Adler Publishers Inc., 1986. This is an excellent work on the effect of worldview bias on reporting. It is must reading for the advanced newshound.

Lichter, S. Robert and Robert E. Noyes of the Center for Media and Public affairs. **Good Intentions Make Bad News**. Published by Rowman & Littlefield, Inc. in 1995.

Lippman, Walter. ***Public Opinion***. London: The Free Press, 1965.

Reston, James. ***The Artillery of the Press***. New York: Harper & Row, 1966.

Rowse, Author E. ***Slanted News***. Boston: Beacon Press, 1957. "A case study of bias in news placement and headline treatment in a presidential campaign."

Rusher, William A. ***The Coming Battle for the Media***. New York: William Morrow and Company, Inc., 1988.

Sanford, Gregory and Vigilante, Richard. ***Grenada: The Untold Story***. New York: Madison Books, 1984.

Schudson, Michael. ***Discovering the News***. New York: Basic Books, 1978. This book provides the Liberal version of the history of journalism.

Shaw, Donald L. and Maxwell E. McCombs. ***The Emergence of American Political Issues: The Agenda-Setting Function of the Press***. Los Angles:

West Publishing Co., 1977. This is the original work which established agenda-setting as a power of the press.

Siebert, Fred S., Theodore Patterson, and Wilbur Schramm. *Four Theories of the Press*. Urbana, Ill.: University of Illinois Press, 1956. "The classic categorization of the operational press theories." This little book describes the social responsibility theory of the press.

Stein, Robert. *Media Power: Who is shaping your picture of the world?*. Houghton Mifflin, 1972.

Stocking, S. Holly and Paget H. Gross. *How Do Journalists Think?* ERIC Clearinghouse on Reading and Communications Skills. Bloomington, Indiana, 1989. This excellent little book surveys the academic literature which, when taken together, strongly suggests that the news is influenced by the opinions and beliefs of journalists.

Weaver, David H. et.al. *Media Agenda-Setting in a Presidential Election*. New York: Praeger, 1981.

INDEX

abortion 25, 43, 74, 128
Accuracy In Media 10
advertising 98, 99
agenda-setting 118, 126
anti-abortionist 26, 43, 79, 128
attack journalism 85, 86, 178
blame 1, 48, 86, 122, 123, 125
Brokaw, Tom -i-, 89
Bush, George 3, 4, 7, 28, 30, 51, 56, 67, 69, 85, 87, 90, 100, 113, 118
Camelot 49
Clinton, William 16, 27, 32, 49, 51, 53, 55, 56, 60, 65, 67, 68, 87-90, 100, 116, 122, 130, 143, 151, 154-156, 180
cognitive matching 22
Conservative 1, 4, 7, 8, 10, 14, 16, 26, 33, 34, 51, 66, 69, 71, 75-77, 92, 102, 108, 112, 118, 128, 140, 169, 170, 177, 185, 187
Couric, Katie 50
Cuomo, Kerry Kennedy 50
decade of greed 24, 27, 51
discriminatory practice 15, 83, 91
double standard 13, 84, 85, 91, 122, 157, 172, 173
fact 34, 75, 148, 162, 163
    defined 1
favoritism 83, 119, 158, 174
flack 88
flack journalism 85, 88-90
frame 74, 128, 143, 151, 156
Gingrich, Newt 50, 85, 91, 105, 124, 129
Hill, Anita 4, 148, 155
Horton, Willy 57, 59, 104
in-group 3
    defined 17
intolerance 1, 8
Iran/Contra 55, 87, 139, 142, 151, 161
Jennings, Peter 118, 175
Johnson, Lyndon 68, 89
Jones, Paula 155, 156
Kennedy, John 49, 93

Kennedy, Robert 49
Liberal 1, 4, 5, 8, 10, 14, 16, 18, 23, 26, 33, 34, 41, 42, 49, 53, 62, 65, 66, 68, 71, 74, 76, 78, 84, 92, 96, 106, 112, 118, 132, 133, 140, 146, 162, 164, 168, 169, 177, 185
Libertarian 14, 18, 34, 69, 75, 77, 92, 108, 128, 140, 169, 170, 185, 186
    defined 186
Limbaugh, Rush 8, 77, 163
MacNeil/Lehrer News Hour 9, 29, 56
media bias 14, 24, 55, 62, 107, 176
muckraking 95-97, 138, 181
Myers, Lisa 53
name-calling 8
New Deal 68, 89
Nixon 109
Nixon, Richard 100, 101, 109
October Surprise 17, 24, 26, 29-31, 146, 150, 160
ordinary Americans 87
out-group 2, 48
    defined 17
partisan gaffe watch 86
partisan mandate 48
pluralistic 14, 92, 98, 118, 169
political fiction 5, 9, 36, 115, 117, 122
Populist 14, 18, 34, 75, 77, 108, 140, 169, 170
prejudice 14, 15, 22, 24, 28, 83, 92, 107, 122, 134, 158, 168, 176
    defined 1
priming 121, 126
quality 168, 171
Quayle, Dan 56, 61, 86, 121
Rather, Dan 78, 87, 90, 151, 175
Reagan, Ronald 30, 38, 48, 49, 51, 59, 88, 117, 142
Ringer 132, 182
Roosevelt, Franklin 68, 89, 111
Roosevelt, Theodore 95
scandal 32, 37, 87, 93, 100, 107, 122, 138-141, 143, 145, 147, 150-152, 158, 173
scandalmongering 138, 142, 181, 182
short term memory 21
spin 39, 88, 103, 104, 107, 111, 112, 123, 126, 127, 133, 134, 146, 160, 183

Thomas, Clarence 4, 56, 148, 155
truth 5, 14, 24, 33, 34, 54, 57, 59, 79, 113, 134, 162-164, 166-168, 172, 174, 176
truth squad 10, 13, 99
us versus them attitude 48, 61, 97, 128, 149
Vietnam War 10, 86
Vietnam: A Television History 11
Watergate 82, 100, 143
xenophobia 10, 119

ENNIS AND NANCY HAM LIBRARY
ROCHESTER COLLEGE
800 WEST AVON ROAD
ROCHESTER HILLS, MI 48307

ROCHESTER COLLEGE
MUIRHEAD LIBRARY
800 WEST AVON ROAD
ROCHESTER HILLS, MI 48307